THINKING OUTSIDE THE BOX... ABOUT LOVE

**Courage to love
and walk through the gate!**

Donna Kasik

GreenWine Family Books™
A division of GlobalEdAdvancePress
www.globaledadvance.org

THINKING OUTSIDE THE BOX... ABOUT LOVE

Copyright © 2009 by Donna Kasik

Library of Congress Control Number: **2009921754**
    Kasik, Donna, 1961–
        Thinking Outside the Box... About Love
            Courage to Love and Walk Through the Gate

ISBN 978-1-935434-00-9
        Subject Codes and Description: 1: REL012010: Religion: Christian Life- Death, Grief, Bereavement; 2. FAM014000: Family & Relationships: Death, Grief, Bereavement; 3. SOC 036000: Social Science: Death and Dying.

All rights reserved, including the right to reproduce this book or any part thereof in any form, except for inclusion of brief quotations in a review, without the written permission of the author and GlobalEdAdvance Press.

Cover Design by Barton Green

Printed in the United States of America

Published by
GreenWine Family Books™
A division of GlobalEdAdvancePress
www.globaledadvance.org

Dedication

This book is dedicated to Richard
Who gave me the courage to love...
Even when we had no idea
What was waiting around the corner.
Thank you, Richard!
It was an honor and a privilege to care for you.
I will always love you with a love that
Even the angels covet.

I want to give a special thanks
To Professor Joshua Collins, Author
Of the book The Knowledge of Good and Evil,
Regarding the immense amount of work
He conducted on my original manuscript,
Which is vastly different from this final book.
I am greatly and humbly thankful.

Table of Contents

Foreword   **11**

Introduction: A Cosmic Game of Chess   **13**

I am a pawn who is treasured by God, and loved beyond human comprehension by my Master and Creator. I was not the queen; a pawn can be used quite effectively in the hands of the Master, despite restricted movements. It is amazing how all the pieces on the Master's side of the board work together in harmony for the collective benefit of the whole, but only in exacting the loving will of the Master.

Chapter 1   Courage to Love the Dying   **17**

This book is about a decision I made that some people found way outside the box, and which actually caused great heartache for me as it altered some of my close relationships. These strained relationships also greatly interfered with my ongoing grief work and complicated the healing process beyond that which I am sure my loved ones knew or could have understood.

Chapter 2   Preparation to Serve Others   **29**

Chicago is home for me. Deserted to raise my son alone, I earned a living by factory work for three years, then a preschool/church janitor for one year. I spent three years in a Trade school to learn the painting trade and worked in the Painter's Union for ten years before starting and operating my own business for ten years. During this time, in addition to raising my son, I went to night school for eight years to earn a bachelor's degree in philosophy; then to seminary for a

Master's in Divinity. Plans were to move to Kentucky to work on a doctorate, but God had other plans. I became a hospital chaplain and began my ministry serving others.

Chapter 3   Thinking about Dying Alone   53

One patient who made an impression on me was named Richard. He became my friend and was like a brother. I believe the reason I became a chaplain at a Veterans hospital was for Richard to find true salvation and finally understand Christ's love and the compassion of others so he would not die alone.

Chapter 4   Laying Down Our Lives   77

We need to lay down our lives daily for our friends. We must love others, even when we do not know what is around the corner. We need to love deeply without thinking about what we can get out of the relationship for ourselves. We love because we are commanded to love, and we love for the sake of others.

Chapter 5   Thinking about a Terminal Diagnosis   101

I loved my dog, Millie, that cute, little goofy dog that I had for only a few months. And I loved Richard who had a thirst for life in spite of a terminal diagnosis that was taking him away despite my prayers and loving care for his illness. Richard too would only be in my life a few months.

Chapter 6   Walking Through the Gate   129

The hospital called; a family was about to remove a patient from life support, and he was expected to die quickly. I went to the hospital and ministered to the family and stayed with them when the life support was removed. It seemed like hours, although only ten minutes passed until the patient

Table of Contents 9

died. The wife could not bear to step through the door and watch him die. The next day was to be their forty-fifth wedding anniversary. The patient had small cell lung cancer, just like Richard. After the final paperwork, I walked out the hospital door and realized that soon I would have to walk through that gate.

Chapter 7   Learning about Turning Stones   157

When I read about "turning stones," it was not clear what the author meant. Near the end of Marc Parent's book, he wrote about a nun traveling in remote places who turned over stones as she went. Someone asked why she turned over stones, and her response opened my eyes. She explained that turning over a stone was a tangible way to say something is different because she was here. I think about her response often. Should not places and people be different because we were there? It is never too late to turn over a stone in someone's life, even in their dying days.

Chapter 8   Thinking Outside the Box   181

A wise man told me that God works outside the box. After reflection, I agree. I began this book by stating that I think outside the box. Do not misunderstand – I am not comparing myself to God. I believe that when we are open minded God will cause us to think outside the box, since He works in ways that are generally contrary to human reasoning and actions. Scripture is clear: "Do not be conformed to this world, but be transformed by the renewing of your minds, so that you may discern what is the will of God – what is good and acceptable and perfect" (Romans 12:2).

References   187

Post Script: Home at Last Animal Sanctuary   189

"**Thinking Outside the Box... About Love**" **by Donna Kasik is the story of one woman's courageous leap of deep faith. Listening to God's voice, she answers the call to a journey that is at times heartwarming, romantic and heartbreaking. It is a bold venture that will challenge your concepts of Christian love and charity. Supported by ample Biblical references, Kasik's straightforward narrative of her life, thoughts and feelings is tender and deeply personal.**

-- Howard Emerson, CMP

Foreword

Come taste and see that the Lord truly is good. He is there, even in the darkest valley of the shadow of death, where peace is the final victory. He is there when love bursts through the midnight hours, though in solitude and sadness.

Richard suffered from many illnesses such as hepatitis B and C, hypertension, acute renal failure, endocarditis, diabetes, depression, and drug addiction, but he was dying of small cell lung cancer. As a hospital chaplain who saw a depressed, lonely man dying alone, with no family and few friends, yet this man was amazingly kind, gentle, humble, loving, polite, considerate... and scared; what was I to do?

Did God call me from my home of over four decades to a "foreign" place in order to help a man live and die? Yes, I felt that Call in my heart! Richard, a wonderful human being, taught me what it means to sacrifice and to love. Through my experiences with this gentleman, I began to learn what Jesus meant when He said to love "one of the least of these" (Matthew 25), and why His ministry was to the lost.

The following pages tell a story of God's amazing grace and love that are "outside the box." You will witness a first-hand account of why Jesus taught that those who have been forgiven much love much (Luke 7). Richard was this kind of man. He had a heart of gold, although he never really knew how to love until the end of his life. Richard's last days clearly demonstrated – it's never too late to learn and to teach others. Thank you, Richard, for your gracious strength, dignified humility, and steadfast love.

"There is no greater love than this,
that a man lay down his life
for the sake of his friends"
--John 15:13

Introduction
A Cosmic Game of Chess

I am a pawn who is treasured by God, and loved beyond human comprehension by my Master and Creator. I was not the queen; a pawn can be used quite effectively in the hands of the Master, despite restricted movements. It is amazing how all the pieces on the Master's side of the board work together in harmony for the collective benefit of the whole, but only in exacting the loving will of the Master.

Relinquish control to the Master

Consider life as a cosmic game of chess. It is easy to assume that we ourselves are master chess players who are able to confront an opposition we take all too lightly. After a few audacious moves, we often find our arsenal greatly diminished. After several reactionary defensive maneuvers, we often find ourselves in check. Seeing only a couple of small and seemingly pathetic options aimed at escaping check momentarily, we come to a decision: either relinquish our control to the Master Chess Player, or invite an impending checkmate.

If we are willing to humble ourselves and admit error, it is then, and only then, that we might take part in the true game that was originally intended for us by the Master; in this sense, we can then become the pieces that the Master moves in order to exact His victorious will. If we accept the status of a pawn, it is amazing to behold how the Master can use a lowly piece to defeat a great one. Yet, the methods of the Master require a refined method as to *how* an apparently lowly pawn is used in order for such a piece to advance towards victory. Any chess piece is but the servant of the Master who wields it. Any piece that confuses itself with the Master is the first to be captured. However, any piece that knows it is only a piece can be used according to the Master's will and can ultimately learn about love, grace, and selflessness, in a manner outside the box.

I am a pawn who is treasured by God, and loved beyond human comprehension by my Master and Creator. Once I understood that I was a pawn, I was able to watch the game unfold and move about the board as needed in order to bring me to the proper squares and to accomplish that which God wanted me to do. The movements were often difficult and confusing, as I seemed to wander from job to job and state to state, but in perfect timing, I arrived at a place where I learned the lessons about love, grace, and selflessness from a dying man.

I did not understand how the game was unfolding, nor could I make sense of my own personal experiences. I found that some of my greatest motivations for movement came through discontentment and seemingly indiscernible events. However, things became much clearer once I realized that my life was not to be lived for myself, and that I was only one piece on the Master's side of the game. I was not the queen; a pawn can be used quite effectively in the hands of the Master, despite its' restricted movements. It is amazing how all of the pieces on the Master's side of the board work together in harmony for the collective benefit of the whole, but only in exacting the loving will of the Master.

Introduction: A Cosmic Game of Chess

The Master's movements often seem atypical, but they are always motivated by His love for His pieces. Perspective is a key to triumph. From a piece's point of view, the motivations for the movements can appear to be restricted to the confines of the board's four corners. A piece can feel boxed in. Yet, it is the will of the Master that moves the pieces, and this will does not stand on the square board itself, but is contemplated from outside of the board. Through love, the Master desires a broader perspective, a view from outside the box, and as the pawn submits to the Master's moves, the pawn then also begins to think and see outside the box. It was in my submission that I began to think about love outside the box.

"....Lord, increase my faith. Bless my efforts, and my work, now and forever."

--Mother Teresa

Chapter One

Courage to Love the Dying

This book is about a decision I made that some people found way outside the box, and which actually caused great heartache for me as it altered some of my close relationships. These strained relationships also greatly interfered with my ongoing grief work and complicated the healing process beyond that which I am sure my loved ones knew or could have understood.

The Courage to Love a Dying Man
I have always thought outside the box, though not always concerning love. Nevertheless, I admit that I do not think like most people I know; that does not bother me, though it sometimes isolates me. After much prayer, mental wrestling, and counsel, I decided to take Richard, a sick and dying man, to my home to care for him until his impending death. First of all, I want to thank those of you who encouraged me, thanked me, and were "proud" of me for caring for Richard. Your love and emotional support were invaluable, and I could not have done it without that occasional pat on the back and kind words, especially as I grew quite weary. I am so very, very thankful to the staff of the Hospice organization who did

all they could to make it possible for Richard to stay in my home until his death, and for helping and encouraging me throughout such a difficult process. Without the help of the nurse, the social worker, and the chaplain, I do not know if I would have been able to let Richard die in the comfort and love of my home.

A Veteran's Hospital Chaplain
I am a chaplain. At the time of this story's unfolding, I worked at a Veteran's hospital in the south, which was quite a different environment for me considering that I was born, raised, and had lived in the Chicago area for over four decades. When I was hired at this Veteran's hospital, I had no suspicion that my life would have turned out as it did. For those of you who have ever been caretakers of a terminally ill person, whether family or friend, you know how extremely difficult it is watching a human being made in the image of God (Genesis 1:27) die. Taking care of Richard was one of the hardest and most painful things I have ever done – but I did it with no regrets.

There are so many melancholy, gut-wrenching, painful life-stories that go unseen, unheard, and unknown. There are so many beautiful human beings who sacrifice and endure the most ardent circumstances, trials, and difficulties, who saunter unrecognized, unloved, and who are dismissed in this life as being but negligible souls passing for an instant on the earth. Of the subtle wonders that the Good Lord enwraps in each person He makes, this book tells the story of one man who almost left this earth unrecognized, unloved, and dismissed...

Sorrowful Casualties of War
We have all heard of gruesome and sorrowful casualties of war, as soldiers fight, suffer, and often die for causes and situations outside of their control. There are elegant recounts of war heroes who stood out above their comrades; but what

of those heroes who had no comrades to stand out above, who were placed in circumstances of isolation where their valiant hearts were not recounted among the noble because no one was there to observe and remember them? What of the unspoken casualties of war that endure *after* war? What of internal scars that never fade when all of the physical fighting is over... scars that are carried for a life time? What of those who, after having been trained to kill heartlessly and fight dauntlessly, are then thrown back into civilian life with no family, friends, hopes, or direction? This book records the memory of Richard – an isolated, rejected, and troubled casualty of war. Richard was a man who was called upon to fight courageously, trained to kill heartlessly, and after such extended brutality, never learned to cope with the casualties of war that endure *after* war.

As many veterans, Richard sought to escape his own private turmoil through substance abuse. He enlisted in the army during wartime out of a patriotism that he termed, "...like mom, apple pie, and the American way." Richard wanted to serve his country, and he laid his private, civilian security aside so that others might retain their private, civilian security. Unfortunately, his transition from an honorable soldier of the American Army back to mom and apple pie was not successful. Mom died, and the apple pie he had once looked forward to began to taste bitter... a taste that led to nearly two decades of imprisonment under the same government he once risked his life for.

We civilians who have never risked our lives for any cause, who do not understand deadly fear, who have never been commanded to take a human life without flinching or regretting, often have difficulty understanding those who do. When we civilians experience our measures of difficulty, we often get together with friends who understand, and perhaps we may discuss our problems over a simple glass of wine.

However, for those soldiers who do understand the hardships that we civilians never will, soldiers who have no friends to get together with, soldiers whose last remaining friends have been slaughtered on the battlefield, may sit alone and cope with methods more potent than a glass of wine. Because of his inability to forget the screams that he remembered, horrors he would never discuss with others, Richard – in isolation – turned to the friendless, hopeless, and destructive world of drugs. Who would ever have assumed that a gentle, humble, young man would risk his own life for those who could never thank him for his heroism, would become a stoic soldier of the United States Army, but would eventually transform into a directionless resident of a United States penitentiary.

As a chaplain at a Veteran's hospital, I was astounded at the number of staff members who inwardly despised many of the soldiers, who, though now troubled, once sacrificed significant portions of their lives for those who now reject them. It was hard to believe the cold and indifferent attitudes and statements harbored by some of those government employees who were supposed to care for such people. Jesus said:

When the Son of Man comes in His glory, and all the angels with Him, then He will sit on the throne of His glory. All the nations will be gathered before Him, and He will separate people one from another as a shepherd separates the sheep from the goats, and He will put the sheep at His right hand and the goats at His left. Then the King will say to those at His right hand, 'Come, you that are blessed by My Father, inherit the kingdom prepared for you from the foundation of the world; for I was hungry and you gave Me food, I was thirsty and you gave Me something to drink, I was a stranger and you welcomed Me, I was naked and you gave me clothing, I was sick and you took care of Me, I was in prison and you visited Me.' Then the righteous will answer Him, 'Lord, when was it that we saw You hungry and gave You food, or thirsty and gave

You something to drink? And when was it that we saw You a stranger and welcomed You, or naked and gave You clothing? And when was it that we saw You sick or in prison and visited You?' And the King will answer them, 'Truly I tell you, just as you did it to **one of the least of these** who are members of My family, you did it to Me.' Then He will say to those at His left hand, 'You that are accursed, depart from Me into eternal fire prepared for the devil and his angels; for I was hungry and you gave Me no food, I was thirsty and you gave Me nothing to drink, I was a stranger and you did not welcome Me, naked and you did not give Me clothing, sick and in prison and you did not visit Me.' Then they also will answer, 'Lord, when was it that we saw you hungry or thirsty or a stranger or naked or sick or in prison, and did not take care of You?' Then He will answer them, 'Truly I tell you, just as you did not do it to **one of the least of these,** you did not do it to Me.' And these will go away into eternal punishment, but the righteous into eternal life (Matthew 25:31-46).

Unable to Adjust to Civilian Life
Unable to adjust to civilian life after Vietnam, Richard found himself scorned and isolated, unable to deal with the suffering he brought home from overseas. Struggling to recapture the "mom, apple pie, and the American way" he once savored and felt obligated to achieve, he estranged himself from those few people who may have been there for him. As a result, some staff members at the Veteran's hospital I worked at looked at a man like Richard as if he did not deserve anything more in this life. They considered him "one of the least of these" in society, as if he was more of a burden than anything else; even the thought of taking care of Richard was burdensome to them. I was told by the woman in charge of palliative care, "Look at him. He looks like an old man since he abused himself all of his life." Was she in a position to make that type of blanket-judgment on him (or any other patient for that matter)? What did his appearance have to do with his

dignity? Ironically, she must not have known Richard's age, as everyone guessed him to be about 45 years old, when, in fact, he was 60.

The cold, cruel attitudes and statements of those whose professions I thought were supposed to be positions of sheepish care were in actuality, heartless, goat-like dismissals of the individuals who needed the most care. The "official" or so called "professional" treatment of human life as negligible refuse intensified my compassion for those entangled in adversity. The judgmental neglect of soldiers like Richard drew me closer to those who were otherwise alone. When I discovered that Richard was basically homeless, and when I continued to hear the pompous words of "professional" caretakers of the hospital in which I worked, I then decided to take Richard home and care for him myself.

Alone and Rejected
Having spent most of his life alone and rejected, compounded with the fact that he was a gunner in an unpopular war, I wanted Richard to get one final glimpse of compassion, tenderness, and forgiveness on this earth before he died. I trusted that my decision to allow Richard to die in my home was the Christian thing to do based on Jesus' teaching as recorded in Matthew 25:31-46. Richard suffered from depression for most of his life. He thought very little of himself because he was repeatedly told that he was nothing more than a junkie and an ex-con who merely took up space on this earth and who contributed nothing. Richard was a man whom the doctors were just waiting for to die. I wanted Richard to know that he was a human being who was made in the image of God (Genesis 1:27), who was as important to God as any other person on earth, who mattered to God, and who could teach and contribute things to other people. He was a person of worth, as we all are. Unfortunately, society told him otherwise, which gave him little desire to change his self-destructive

ways. I did not want Richard to die thinking negatively about himself, nor did I want him to die an addict. Thanks to God – Richard did not die an addict or with a negative outlook.

While I cared for him, Richard lived in the knowledge that he was loved unconditionally by my son, some friends, my church, and me, with all of his flaws and weaknesses. Through the power of prayer, the grace of God, and unconditional love, Richard was able to overcome his addiction and self-defeating perspectives. Richard overcame his depression while living in my home, except for the normal sadness that accompanies most people when they know they are dying and are not ready to go. He did regain his self-esteem and he understood the he was loved, and the love he gave to others unconditionally was treasured as well.

I do not believe people should die alone in some type of institution, if such a circumstance is avoidable. As is the practice of Hospice, I believe that people should be able to die at home, whether home is with family members or with friends, and that they should die surrounded by someone, anyone, who loves them; unfortunately all do not have such an opportunity. While the Hospice service I utilized did have an inpatient facility, as I believe most do, that facility was reserved for those people who had no option, and I am thankful such facilities exist. However, I believed that Richard did have an option, which was my home.

Codes of Ethics and Rules
Hospitals and various institutions have their codes of "ethics" and rules, which usually deny someone like Richard the opportunity to live and die with an employee such as myself. I looked upon the opportunity for Richard to die in a home with a friend who cared for him (and not alone in an institution) as the grace, purpose, and plan of God that allowed one final measure of human love. I think the rules and ethical

codes that restrict compassion for those in need must be re-examined as to their purpose; if those rules are more important than human life, then they need to be challenged. I have no inherent problems with authority or rules, as the Bible tells us to obey those in authority over us (Romans 13). I understand that rules and ethical codes are intended for protective reasons, but I also believe there are times when such rules need to be challenged when those rules do not affect the intended causes. When various rules defy their own purpose, exceptions can and should be made for the good of a person or people. While Scripture establishes many clear codes of ethics and rules (Matthew 25), they are all based on love and compassion for others. When we love God and our neighbor as ourselves, we would naturally want to feed the hungry, give a drink to the thirsty, welcome a stranger, clothe the naked, and *care for the sick.*

The Rules of Segregation
What if no one challenged the rules of segregation? What if Dr. Martin Luther King Jr. and all others who were part of the Civil Rights Movement admitted that the laws of segregation were there for a protective purpose and should not be challenged? What if Jesus never challenged anyone to examine their hearts and motives regarding the various rules and ethical codes that were harshly placed upon so many people (but were not found in the Scriptures) without considering the effects those official (but non-Scriptural) rules had on people?

Any rule or ethical code that supersedes love and compassion is a rule that needs to be re-examined and challenged. Please do not misunderstand my motivation; I did not take Richard into my home to challenge the "system." Actually, I did not even know at the time that such a rule that forbade a man in Richard's position from living and dying in my home was in existence. I never hid the fact that he was to be cared for in my home, as the remainder of this book will illustrate. I did nothing out of an impure motive. I did not want to challenge authority. I took Richard home because I thought my action was something Jesus would have done. Christian love, my faith in God, and my compassion for "one of the least of these" were my only motivations for allowing Richard to stay in my home. I hope this record of an almost forgotten human being, an honorable veteran, but a rejected man, will illustrate why such care and consideration is necessary for all of God's children – even those who are considered the least of those children.

I admire Mother Teresa, who acted Christ-like probably more than any person I can remember. I also try to be like Christ as much as possible, as we are commanded, though I fall far short. Mother Teresa wrote a prayer at the end of her book *No Greater Love,* that I think sums up how I initially saw Richard and why I took him home with me. Here is her prayer:

"O Jesus"

You who suffer, grant that, today and every day,
I may be able to see you in the person of your sick ones
and that, by offering them my care, I may serve you.
Grant that, even if you are hidden under the
unattractive disguise of anger, of crime, or of madness,
I may recognize you and say, "Jesus, you who suffer,
how sweet it is to serve you."

Give me, Lord, this vision of faith,
and my work will never be monotonous,
I will find joy in harboring the small whims
and desires of the poor who suffer.

Dear sick one, you are still more beloved to me
because you represent Christ. What a privilege I am
granted in being able to take care of you!

> O God, since you are Jesus who suffers,
> deign to be for me also a Jesus who is patient,
> indulgent with my faults, who looks only at my intentions,
> which are to love you and to serve you in the person of each
> of these children of yours who suffer.
>
> Lord, increase my faith. Bless my efforts, and my
> work, now and forever. (Mother Teresa 183).

Read this book without preconceived notions, and with an open mind. I am sure there are some readers who will disagree with me and my actions; that is fine. We can agree to disagree, and I respect your opinions. For those of you who do agree with my decisions and actions, I hope you find comfort in knowing Richard died a changed man because he was cared for, and that he is in Heaven today because God loved him. As for me, I grew and learned many things from Richard as I walked with him on his road to death, and I am still learning as I continue on the sometimes painful, surprising, and wonderful journey of life.

"Do nothing from selfishness or empty conceit, but with humility of mind let each of you regard one another as more important than himself; do not merely look out for your own interests, but also for the interests of others."

–Philippians 2:3-4

Chapter Two

Preparation to Serve Others

Chicago is home for me. Deserted to raise my son alone, I earned a living by factory work for three years, then a preschool/church janitor for one year. I spent three years in a Trade school to learn the painting trade and worked in the Painter's Union for ten years before starting and operating my own business for ten years. During this time, in addition to raising my son, I went to night school for eight years to earn a bachelor's degree in philosophy; then to seminary for a Master's in Divinity. Plans were to move to Kentucky to work on a doctorate, but God had other plans. I became a hospital chaplain and began my ministry serving others.

My Life in Illinois
The Chicago area is my home. Prior to coming to know Jesus and understanding a walk with Christ, at age 19 I gave birth to my son. Shortly after my sons' birth, his father left, and he never supported us in any way. Needless to say, I was poor for quite a few years. When my son was one month old, I went to work in a factory for three years, and then as a pre-school/ church janitor for the next year. I soon realized that I was on a

dead end street and would always be poor. Frustrated, unfulfilled, and bored, I decided to go into the construction trades since I knew I would be able to at least make more money and obtain some benefits such as health insurance for my son and me.

I went to Trade school for the next three years to learn the painting trade, which was not a welcoming environment for women. In Trade school I began as an apprentice and worked four days per week as I went to school one full day per week (while I made little money), but I knew every few months, I would receive a pay raise. I was able to make this financial sacrifice because, within three years, I would become a journeyman painter and would then be making good money to support us. I did well as a painter in the construction business, and after working in the Painter's Union in Chicago for over ten years, I decided to start my own painting business, which I had for the next ten years. My prosperity increased yearly and I soon got used to *not* being poor.

During the time that I was working in the painting trade, I decided at age twenty-nine to get a college degree, since I could not see myself retiring as a construction painter. Physical labor is difficult after many years, especially for women, as it is hard on the body. I worked a lot of overtime in order to pay for night school without going into debt. Going to school part-time at night is a long process. After eight years, I finally earned my bachelor's degree in philosophy. During those years in college, and wondering what exactly I would do with a philosophy degree, I felt called to go to seminary to pursue a Masters of Divinity degree.

While in seminary, one of my learning goals was to just "be" with God, as my hectic 80 to 90 hour per week schedule precluded me from doing that; I was a single mom who worked, ran a painting business, and went to night school for fifteen years part time to earn both my bachelors degree and then my masters degree from seminary. During that time period, I was given a book written by Brother Lawrence entitled, *The Practice of the Presence of God,* which I devoured and only now am beginning to understand. I was finally learning now to just "be" with God, and it was good.

As strange as it seemed to me, while I was getting close to graduating from seminary, I felt called to move to Kentucky, which was quite a transition from what I was accustomed to over the last four decades. I graduated from seminary with plans of working on my Doctorate at a seminary in Kentucky. I closed a successful painting business in Illinois, sold my house, and moved to Kentucky since that is where I felt God calling me. My son did not want to move to Kentucky, but he told me that he would help me get settled and then he would go back to Illinois. I was upset, as I wanted to at least live in the same state as my son. For many parents, and probably more so for single parents, letting go of our children is difficult, even though we raise them to give them wings and live their own lives, yet I thought we could live in the same state and still live independently, which was my desire. However, I was the one who felt that I should leave Illinois. My decision to go was difficult. At the same time, I felt sure of this move with no doubts about it whatsoever, but it hurt to think that I would be living in Kentucky and my son would be living in Illinois.

House Hunting in Kentucky
When I knew I was to leave the Chicago area and move to Kentucky, I had no idea where I was going to live or how this move would work out. I did not have a job in Kentucky, and I had no idea how long it would take to find one. I did not know what salary I would earn in this new state, so I was determined to pay for a house in cash and to be debt free. Now it was time to find a house in Kentucky which I wrongly assumed would be simple. It did not turn out to be as simple as I thought, even though houses are far less expensive in Kentucky than they

are in the Chicago suburbs. The houses in the price range that I wanted to stay in were terrible. I wanted something decent that I did not have to put any money into repairing in order to make livable. I went to Kentucky three times and never found a house that would give me what I needed, or that met the requirements I actually wanted, which were two bedrooms, one bathroom, a fenced in yard for my dogs, and either a garage or a basement for storage.

The only homes I found in Kentucky that were in my price range were townhouses, which I did not want, which had no yard or storage space whatsoever, and which also had monthly fees. What was I going to do? Appearing to have no choice but to buy a townhouse, I decided on one and I told my realtor that I was ready to buy, since I had to get back to Chicago soon. She told me she was busy, and since we were both tired, she suggested that I sleep on it and then make a final decision the next day. I agreed since her suggestion sounded reasonable.

That afternoon I prayed, "God, I don't like anything I saw, and I still am not 100% sure what to buy, even though I think I made a decision. Show me what I should buy and where I should live." As I sat in my car praying, I was prompted by the Lord to turn left over a hill that went out into the country. I had never driven in that direction before because it did not appear to go anywhere; but I obeyed His voice, as I am learning to do more and more. After driving a block or so, there it was – the house that suited me perfectly! I pulled into the driveway and called the phone number on the sign in the front yard, and I discovered that the house was $5,000 less than my top price that I was willing to pay. Being a painter for over twenty years, I also did not want a house whose exterior needed to be painted. Not only was this entire house vinyl, but the cute white fence on the side was vinyl as well. One problem – the house was for sale by owner, and my realtor had been working with me for nine months. I thought I would look at it first to see if this was the house (though I already knew it was), and then pray about how to handle the situation. My dad had come with me on this particular house-hunting trip, so I went back to the motel where he was resting and told him about the house. We made plans to look at this house that same evening when the homeowner/seller got in from work.

Six o'clock came, and when we walked in that house, my dad and I looked at each other and knew this was it. The house was in perfect shape and the price was right. It had two bedrooms, one bathroom, a fenced in yard, and a large garage, just what I needed. I then had to call the realtor. I told her about it, and we settled on my paying a percentage of the sale price to her as her pay for the work she had done for me over the past nine months. Remembering how perfectly organized God is, and how perfect His timing is, I knew I should never have doubted that He would assist me in finding the right house in Kentucky, which of course He did.

After purchasing this house in Kentucky, I returned to Illinois and began packing. Once I was all packed, I led a caravan of vehicles: my son drove one moving truck, I drove another moving truck, my twin sister drove my son's car and my dad drove my van. We all headed south, as I left with tearful good byes in Illinois to my friends and neighbors of many years.

Settling Into my New Home
When we finally arrived in Kentucky, my son said that he liked my little house in my new home-state, and he decided to stay for a while, which made me happy. My son and I both took the next several months and just relaxed, explored, and tried to discern God's will. I had just graduated from college and seminary after fifteen years of night school; while attending school part time, working a huge surplus of hours each week, running my own business and raising my son alone as a single

mom, I was exhausted. Life had been hard and hectic for so many years and I felt I needed a short break. It was wonderful to have this opportunity to do just that, and I will always be most grateful to God.

Life was Good

My son also needed a break from working a lot of hours, which he always worked without complaint in order to help me, while he also went to college and undertook heavy course loads with a broken leg and two unsuccessful surgeries in that time-period. He had been a college basketball player until his leg injury, which ended his athletic career. My son and I explored our new home area and found a favorite spot not far from my house where we could kayak, horseback ride, and enjoy nature. We quickly became friends with the owner of this beautiful resort and we went to this place as often as we could. Soon after my move to Kentucky, I took my annual trip to Kenya to teach at a seminary, and my son took a vacation to Hawaii. Life was good.

A New Church Home

For many reasons God directed us immediately to a church home. The people were unusually friendly. The pastor introduced himself before the service began. This church was a comfortable, casual, non-denominational Christian, charismatic church where I felt much at home. Two men from the church (the associate pastor and an elder) came to visit us at home the same week, and the following Sunday the pastor invited us out to lunch. For my son and I, this church was now family where we quickly made some good friends. This church was the most authentic church I have ever attended and a church I will always consider my church home, no matter where life takes me.

I had been accepted into a Kentucky seminary as a Doctoral student only to discover the full scholarship I was promised never materialized. None of the things promised by this institution were valid! What was I to do, and why was I in Kentucky away from everyone I knew and loved? I still felt God's peace and I knew that Kentucky was where He wanted me... but why? I was angry and confused, yet at that same time I felt what the Bible calls "...the peace of God, which passes all understanding..." (Philippians 4:7); I had it.

Questioning this Move
A few days later I was doing some volunteer work at my church and my pastor asked how I was doing. I told him that I was a bit upset and uncertain as to what I should do, since I did not feel comfortable going through the last of my savings account in order to pay for seminary, nor did I feel comfortable enough to take out hefty loans since I never had to take out loans for my education before. God had always given me work that enabled me to pay for my education as I went along, so for me, I felt that was the plan God had for any future educational pursuits. I still knew I should be in Kentucky, but for what? I thought I came for further education, and since that plan seemed to be falling apart, and I could not find a job, I guess I began to second guess God... did I hear Him wrongly? I was sure that I did not, as I had also left Illinois with much advice and counsel. Pastor Steve, being the great pastor and man of God that he is, put his hand to his mouth with a look of shock, and said, "I guess God had no idea this was going to happen!" Funny and a bit sarcastic as usual, I knew he was trying to make me look at this scenario in a new light in order to trust God with my future plans. I laughed and went home. I prayed. I waited. I looked to see what God was going to do. I soon realized that the Doctoral program in Kentucky is what God used to bring my son and me to this area, though it would be for other reasons yet unknown. I was at peace with this knowledge.

I sent out over fifty resumes and job applications, but I could not find a job. My son decided to stay in Kentucky for a while, since the job he was offered in Illinois dissolved two weeks before he moved me to Kentucky – much to his displeasure. He found a job in Kentucky, and that following year he was awarded a full academic scholarship to the University of Kentucky to get his Masters Degree. At least one of us furthered their education in Kentucky!

Unusual Employment
I finally got a part-time job working about twelve hours a week at an animal sanctuary about thirty miles away from my new home. When I talked to Margie, the owner of the animal sanctuary, she was reluctant to hire me. She said it was a hard dirty job that required taking care of a lot of animals on their 190-acre farm and it involved working outside in all kinds of weather. Furthermore, when she considered the fact that I had a master's degree, she was sure that I would not enjoy working at the sanctuary. I told her that I desperately needed a job, so I asked her again to let me work for her. The pay was $100 per week, and considering the long ride through the country roads cost me about $50 per week in gas, it hardly seemed worth it, but I took the job anyway. I started the job January 31 – a great time to start an outdoor job! I cried the first day of work while I drove there, since I felt like the prodigal son from the Bible (Luke 15) as I prepared to feed pigs on a farm. Yes, I had pigs to feed... in addition to many dogs, cats, a horse, and a rabbit. There were also goats, huge hogs and cows, but the owner's husband, Terry, fed them. After a short time working at the sanctuary three times per week, I fell in love with the farm and the animals, and I got to really love Margie and Terry as well.

Finally a full-time Job
Finally a full time job – at the seminary where I was supposed to be working on my Doctorate! Though I had told Margie and Terry at the animal sanctuary that I was going to quit when

I found full time work, by this time, I had fallen in love with the animals and could not bring myself to leave. Also, when I received my first pay check at the seminary, I earned in two weeks in Kentucky what I made in less than two days in Chicago; with such a huge pay cut, that extra $100 (actually $50) that I earned per week from the farm was needed.

I worked in an office at the seminary. This position was quite strange for me, since I had worked construction most of my occupational life. I was similar to a fish out of water working in an office, with zero office skills. My boss did not have a lot of office skills either since he had always worked as a pastor and had a secretary. We were the blind leading the blind, as it was just the two of us in that particular department. Between the low pay, the confinement of an office and the awkwardness of office work, I was miserable. Although I was thankful for the job, I wondered what on earth I was doing there. I met some wonderful people and developed some good friendships, but I did not think those good things constituted the reason I had this job.

One of my co-workers, with whom I quickly became friends, was going to quit the seminary to start his own business. He asked me repeatedly to work for him, but I repeatedly declined. He and his wife had bought a landscaping business, and since he knew that I had formerly owned and operated a painting business in Chicago, he told me that I would be a great asset to his company as a supervisor. After many persuasive conversations and invitations to their home to discuss this opportunity, I finally agreed to work for him when he offered me $10,000 a year more than I was making at the seminary.

Surely I knew that money was not everything. My friend/co-worker's salary offer was still relatively small, compared to what I was accustomed to making in Chicago, but it would certainly help make ends meet. I worked for this landscaping business for a few days and found that I would not be in any supervisory position as was the initial agreement, but was only doing hard manual labor, which was something that I thought I gave up when I closed my painting business in Illinois. After over twenty years of physical labor, my back was beginning to hurt and I was certainly not getting any younger. I thought those days were behind me, but there they were again.

This new landscaping job was tough, and I really disliked it. I was on my hands and knees pulling weeds. I was shoveling landscape rocks out of trucks, into wheelbarrows, and spreading them in landscape beds. I was shoveling and spreading mulch. I was spraying toxic chemicals to kill weeds, while I was wearing long sleeves in the hot Kentucky sun. I was operating huge lawn mowers that actually scared me, as I had no clue how to operate such machines. I was cutting, hauling, and laying sod. I came home each night hot, filthy, and exhausted. I was so miserable. I regretted this job change so much, and my frustration at the situation grew stronger with each day. After working physical labor my whole life and going to night school to enable myself to stop this type of work, there I was again, with a master's degree working harder than I had for a long time, for a third of the money I had previously made painting. I could have stayed in Chicago and painted if I wanted this life to continue. What on earth had I done?

I talked to my friend/boss about all of the wonderful things he promised me that were not coming true at all and he became angry. Perhaps he thought things would be different than they were. Perhaps he thought since I enjoyed the outdoors that I would actually like this type of work. He promised so many things to me with this job, and those promises prompted me to leave my difficult to get seminary job, but none of his words came true. Things became tense. When the tension, the labor, the hours, and the circumstances began to seem overwhelming, I told him that I wanted to quit. He asked me to stick it out with his company, so, as a friend, I agreed. However, that agreement did not make the awful, dirty job any easier for me, nor did the working conditions improve.

My boss and his wife asked if I really hated the job; I was honest and I expressed my dissatisfaction. They did not seem to care. In retrospect, I guess I hurt their feelings and maybe went about the situation incorrectly, but at the time I thought about how much I hated painting but it was a living. I was always aloof about the idea of enjoying work since I never enjoyed any of my jobs, and to express dissatisfaction about the work was just something most of us did, unfortunately. I only dreamed of a day when I would actually enjoy my job, which I thought after years of education, would finally happen.

I was also surprised that my landscaping bosses had already fired three workers, one of whom was a good friend of theirs whom they had also made promises to but did not keep and he had also expressed his dissatisfaction and was fired for it. They fired more people in three months than I fired in ten years when I had my business! We were all hurt, and my friends gave me the job as if they had done me a favor. I took the job not only for some extra money, but I also thought I was doing them a favor. They began to get quite angry and stopped speaking to me. This silence between us was awkward, since it was just the three of us who usually worked together. One day, in the midst of this hurt and insanity, I asked my boss what was going on, and without stopping what he was doing (changing a wheel on a wheelbarrow) or even looking at me he said, "This is not working out." "No, it is not," I concurred, and I asked him what the next step was to be. He would not answer me. I asked again, and I got the silent treatment. I finally asked, "Are you going to fire me?" To my extreme hurt, he said, "Yes." When I asked him when this would take place, he told me at the end of the month. I was devastated. I had left a low-paying job at the seminary that I did not like and that did not at all fit my skills and talents, but it was steady and secure. Now, after only three months, I was going to lose my job, and to think how long it took for me to get a job in Kentucky... what on earth was I going to do? I immediately called my son, since I began to go into a slight panic and was angry.

To be fired from a job at age 45 was devastating, and the loss of a good friendship complicated being fired. I felt God tell me to do one thing: pray *with* them, by holding their hands, on that last day when they would ask me for the phone and keys to the shop and fire me. I responded, "Lord, you have got to be kidding! I do NOT want to do that!" Two people who were once my friends, who had promised me the moon, and who never came through with any of their promises, were firing me and causing me to lose my income and my health insurance. Then I heard the Lord remind me to love and pray for our enemies, in which it felt to me they had become. In my prayers I told God that I really did not want to pray with them, but out of obedience, I told Him that I would. However, I did ask God to put in my heart to *want* to pray with my two friends/bosses, which would make that act more genuine. Shortly after this prayer, I really did want to be obedient, and I felt a supernatural love for them both that I could never have had on my own.

My last day working for my "friend" finally came. I had a stomach ache all day, but I knew that I needed to pray with them at the end of the day. At 4:00 p.m., the wife of my "friend" who hired me began to smoke a cigarette, which she rarely did, so I knew that she felt a little nervous; she walked away. Her husband, the other owner, was busy sharpening tools, so I thought, "Good – if they are not available, then perhaps I do not have to pray with them after all." I asked

God to let me get out of this prayer, as I was starting to feel not quite up to the task. Maybe I could just leave the keys and phone in the shop and walk away... No such luck and I use that word "luck" loosely. The woman co-owner walked over to me and her husband also came over and looked at me (what an awkward moment). I said, "Here are the keys and the phone." He thanked me and said that he was sorry it came to this. I agreed, and then I asked if I could say a prayer for their business and for them. They both looked at me with some surprise, and said, "Sure." I then held out my hands to them; they hesitated, but they took my hands anyway. I prayed for their business to be successful, for God to be close to them both, and for God to bless all they did. When I said, "Amen," we let go of each others' hands, and I walked away. It was not so hard after all, but I was glad it was over. I felt a burden lift off of my shoulders, and I knew I could have only done that by the grace and power of God.

Fortunately, I was able to apply for unemployment, and I collected a couple of checks until I found part-time work at the University of Kentucky taking care of an incoming student with muscular dystrophy. Unfortunately, this new job paid quite poorly and was only twenty hours per week, so I also went back to working at the animal sanctuary three days per week; I missed the farm and everyone there anyway. It was good to get back to the animals that I loved, and it was good to see Margie and Terry as well, whom I also missed.

With all of these employment problems, I knew that I needed to make some type of move, and that I could not live on such poverty level wages for much longer. I had already gone through some of my savings since I moved to Kentucky, and my financial life was going from bad to worse. I had worked so hard for so long to make a decent living, and now I felt like I had taken two steps forward and ten steps backward. Money is not everything, and I never had a lot of it, but I wanted to be self-sufficient; I wanted, maybe, to go out once in a blue moon and also be able to take my annual Kenya trips to teach, which, at this point, I knew would come to a screeching halt if things did not change. I could not help anyone out financially either, as I had enjoyed doing occasionally in Kenya. I began to pray in earnest and try to figure out what it was that God wanted me to do and why I was experiencing so many difficulties. Surely God is in control and has a plan; I just needed to figure out what it was.

Prayerful Considerations
I continued to pray. I thought about pursuing the call I originally had when I started seminary, which was hospital chaplaincy. I had gotten off track of what I felt God wanted me to do because chaplaincy seemed impossible. While I lived in Illinois, the cost of living was much too high for me to do the required one-year Residency, which paid a low stipend, so I put chaplaincy out of my mind. I thought a PhD was what I should pursue so that I could teach, especially since I loved to teach in Kenya and thought that teaching was my call instead. But the more I thought about the mess I seemed to be in, and the more I prayed about these struggles, the stronger I felt God calling me to chaplaincy. I began to apply for my Clinical Pastoral Education (CPE) with the hopes that I would somehow be able to pull chaplaincy off financially, though I had no idea how this plan might work.

The Veterans hospital in Kentucky appeared interested in my chaplaincy application, but they told me that I would need to complete one more semester of unpaid CPE prior to my one year Residency; I had no idea how I would be able to do that, but I trusted God to provide. The Veterans hospital was the only hospital in the area where I lived that would be able to take me due to administrative problems and a lack of staff in other area hospitals; so, in order to stay in my house, all my eggs were in this one basket. I called the CPE supervisor several times within the next couple of months to confirm that I could begin the program during the upcoming January. I wanted to begin earlier, in September for the Fall unit, but no one would allow me to begin at that time since I had a two-and-a-half week trip booked for Kenya at the end of October into mid November. I called and wrote letters and emails, but I received no response. Finally, I got a phone call and was told that when I came back from Kenya, the supervisor at the Kentucky Veterans' hospital would decide if I could begin my CPE in January. The supervisor's message was frustrating, as I told him that if for some reason I did not get in, all other programs would be filled up and I would have to wait yet another year; what was I going to do in the meantime? I felt like I had already wasted two years half-starving in Kentucky, though I knew God was preparing me and molding me for something for which I was not quite ready.

Even though I *know* God does not waste time, I sometimes have a hard time really believing that fact. It is often difficult to be patient, since human time is vastly different from God's time, and I sometimes "remind" God to remember what it is like to live as one of us within the confines of time! I think of that "prayer" that says, "Lord, give me patience – NOW!" In retrospect, I saw that God causes or allows difficulties and even confusion to occur in order to teach us and mold us into who we need to be for His purpose, to increase our faith and dependence on Him, and to prepare us for our next assignment; He never said it would be easy.

Contemplating another Move
I began to pray in earnest about what to do. Things just did not appear to be working out, and I felt I had to make a major change. In his *Experiencing God* study, Henry Blackaby said, "God's invitation for you to work with Him always leads you to a crisis of belief that requires faith and action" (Blackaby, 2007). I felt like I was at such a crisis and that I needed to take

some action. I talked with my pastor and a former seminary professor about perhaps looking outside of the area where I lived for work. I needed to see what God had in mind for me elsewhere, as Kentucky was becoming a dead end. I was told unanimously by these trusted friends and some family members that I should look in other areas of the country to complete my CPE Residency – so I did. I thought perhaps I should consider the Chicago area since that was my home, and because my friends and family were there. I also applied in Colorado since it is a state that I love more than nearly any other. I applied in several other western states, which was the direction I wanted to move, and also to some states that were relatively close to Kentucky. I did not want to go south. I felt like I was a Northerner, and going even farther south (farther than Kentucky) just did not quite appeal to me. However, I kept hearing God speak to me about applying to another southern state, (which I will refer to as State X for reasons of anonymity and protection). Why on earth would I want to go there? But State X stayed in my mind for several days – so I applied there.

About a week or so later, as I was leaving my job at the university and on my way to the animal sanctuary job for the remainder of the day, my cell phone rang. My phone was always off and I almost never answered it while driving, but I did that day. It was the CPE supervisor from State X, who received my application and was interested in me. I told him I would get back to him when I got home, since I was driving and did not have any information in front of me. To my surprise, when I got home later that day, I had a message on my home phone and also an email as well. I thought, "Surely this guy is interested in me." I emailed and called him again, and once we connected, we set up an interview for later that week. I arranged to take a day off of work and I drove to State X.

The chaplain supervisor in State X was able to see me even

though I arrived quite early, and the interview was short and sweet. If I wanted the job, it was mine – and I accepted! I was so excited, and I immediately called my son to tell him. My son was so happy for me. Before I returned to Kentucky, I first wanted to look around the local neighborhoods and think about where I would live. I was going to keep my house in Kentucky since it was paid-in-full, and also since the position in State X lasted for but one year and I would at least have a home base. I would live in a small apartment while I was working on my CPE Residency. My son agreed to live in my Kentucky house so that I did not have to leave it empty or have the hassle of renting it from another state. To my surprise, the small, one-bedroom apartments near the hospital were expensive and out of my price range. I wondered how I was going to arrange this strange set-up. My new job, along with the necessary adjustments required, appeared to be an opportunity that just fell into my lap. However, even though my new opportunity appeared to be from God, I had no idea how I could afford to pull it off financially.

My son further encouraged me to get out of the Kentucky area that was killing us both financially. I talked to my pastor and a former seminary professor who taught my CPE class while I was in Illinois attending seminary, and I received repeated confirmation that this move to State X was from God and that I should pursue it. I accepted the job and I told my new chaplain supervisor that I would need a few weeks to leave my jobs at the animal sanctuary and at the university (taking care of the girl who had muscular dystrophy), so that they could find replacements. I had grown to love both the animals and the girl I took care of; as excited as I was at my new opportunity, it was also bittersweet.

After I returned to Kentucky, I called my CPE supervisor and told him that I did not know how I would be able to take this job, as the cost of living seemed to prohibit my move to State

X. He steered me in directions of cheaper living, and he told me where to go and where not to go, which was of great help. The Saturday after my interview in State X, I drove down for a second time to the area where I would be working and I asked the Lord to show me where to live. The Lord had shown me where to live in Kentucky, so I knew He would also guide me in State X.

Here We Go Again
The first apartment that I viewed was awful, and my heart sank. However, the second apartment I viewed was exactly what I needed, and the landlord allowed up to two dogs, which I had. The apartment complex was large, well lit, and it had a lot of grassy areas for me to walk my dogs. This complex also had a lot of trees, was on a large river, and had a country feel to it. There was a big patio attached to the first-floor apartment, which I wanted particularly for my dogs. There was also a swimming pool which I was sure I would use, and this particular apartment had parking right outside my patio. The apartment units also had central air conditioning and large, low windows for my dogs to look out during the day. I was dealing with limited funds to set up another home, and this apartment also had a built-in kitchen table so that I did not have to worry about buying a table. God is so organized! This new apartment was only a few minutes drive to work, and the price was acceptable; all was set. I was going to move to State X. I was excited, and God was taking care of everything, just as He did when I left Chicago. God seems to work at the eleventh hour, and by doing so, He constantly builds my faith.

Ordination
My CPE supervisor, named "T" at the hospital where I would soon be working asked me if I was ordained, since he and the hospital chaplaincy program wanted their chaplains to be ordained, primarily so the chaplains could rotate pastoral roles on Sunday morning services and serve the Lord's Supper. I

told T that I would ask my pastor if my church in Kentucky would ordain me. My church is a non-denominational (or inter-denominational) church, and it would be a matter of the leadership agreeing to the ordination.

I called Pastor Steve and told him about the situation of ordination, so he asked me to write a short biography and job description of the chaplain position to submit to the elders. The elders would read my biography, meet with me in order to further assess my capability and Christian calling, and then take a vote. My church had never ordained a woman (with the exception of a husband and wife team) and there were no women on the pastoral staff, nor did any women serve as elders. I placed my situation in God's hands and knew He would work things out. After all of the matters that determined my ordination took place, the vote was unanimous – in favor of my ordination on October 7, and I would be leaving for my new assignment on October 13. I was excited.

My son asked on the morning of my ordination, if I was nervous, to which I replied, "No"; but when asked to speak to the congregation, I was shaking like a leaf. During the ceremony, I actually felt the responsibilities being placed upon me, and recognized more fully that I would be responsible to God for my ministry to the hospital patients and their families. My son bought me a beautiful Bible to celebrate this day, which he proudly personalized. I was truly blessed.

State X

At the time I was planning on moving to State X, I was in the middle of Henry Blackaby's study called, *Experiencing God*, which teaches (among many other things) that, "I can't stay where I am and go with God" (Blackaby, 2007), and this is a principle I quickly learned. God moved me from my home state of Illinois, where all of my family and friends were, to Kentucky, and after two years in Kentucky, He prepared to move me again... alone. Often, when God calls people to various places, it is a solitary journey.

Sure I was nervous. I had the van all packed and was all ready to go. I went outside to warm up the van on this cold morning, and the van would not start! I was scheduled to move on this day and I was to start work two days later. I had no idea what I was going to do. I admit that I panicked, and then I prayed (and the reader will notice the wrong order of things)! I asked my son to jump the battery. He pushed the van to the bottom of the driveway, and to my delight, when we hooked up the cables, it started. I dared not turn the van off until I got to my new apartment. Due to this minor setback, it seemed as if something was trying to stop this move, which caused me to think about how God's plans often come through unexpected difficulties and trials.

God then moved me to State X, which is even farther south than Kentucky. Never in my wildest imagination did I think I would live in the south, especially more than once. Through many trials, and what felt like two years of wandering in the wilderness of Kentucky, I found myself alone in an apartment in State X, while my son took care of my house in Kentucky, even though the Chicago area had always been our home. What in the world was God up to? God never does things the way we would do them, or in a way we would even begin to imagine. "For as the heavens are higher than the earth, so are My ways higher than your ways, and My thoughts than your thoughts" (Isaiah 55:9). God's ways surely are not our ways...for sure, I've read that many times in Scripture, but I found myself living such a reality! I said, "**God** then moved me to State X"; I did not say that **I** moved myself to State X, because when we follow God and live in a close, intimate relationship with Him, He does things and moves us places we never thought we would go. I moved out of my Kentucky house and got an apartment; what a strange turn that was –

the parent moving out of the house and into an apartment! In the process of this move, I understood, more than ever, the importance of friends and family.

Living in Isolation
Being initially isolated in a new state can be quite a rootless and alienating experience, especially when you are accustomed to being with family and friends. Through such an experience, God teaches you to be completely dependent on Him where He develops a more intimate relationship with you, since your only companion for a while may be your Heavenly Father.

After I moved from Kentucky to State X, I found myself *completely* detached from my friends and family. Living with no family, no friends, and no church family was not a situation I expected. For those who do not have family nearby, the church family is so important. I needed to get connected with a good church since I was planning to live by myself and felt the need to get plugged into another family, even though it would be temporary. I would be similar to a foster child. I missed seeing my son often and talking about simple topics such as daily events, conversations we had throughout the day that were interesting, new information learned and shared and such things. A friend from Illinois reminded me that when people get a call from God to go somewhere and do something, His calling often has an insular side to it. Many people are uprooted from friends, family, and even from their own countries, without any apparent support system, and it is during these times that one learns to rely on God completely and learns to practice His presence. God has His way of making us rely completely on Him and not ourselves, and He gives us challenges that will increase our faith. My new situation in State X was going to be a challenge; I could feel it. For the two years that I was in Kentucky, my schedule was lighter than it was when I lived in Chicago, but my schedule became even lighter in State X. In Kentucky, after I finally found work, I always worked several jobs since the pay was so low: I worked at the animal sanctuary, the seminary, and I edited Doctoral Dissertations part-time at the seminary as well; during the interval I worked at the university, I also worked at the farm; while I landscaped, I worked one day per week at the farm. After venturing to State X, God brought me down to only one job – chaplaincy at a hospital – which is what I had wanted to do since I began seminary eight years before.

Having had my income reduced again, I learned again the lesson about the insignificance of material things. However, at this point, I learned so much more, being in the south without pretty much everything, including furniture. Alone in my apartment, I had one wooden desk chair and one wood and canvas Chicago Bulls chair which belonged to my son, though neither piece of furniture was comfortable. I had a small wooden desk, which my son's girlfriend gave me; she also gave me a small wooden nightstand that I placed next to my bed. I missed sitting on a big soft chair or lying down on a couch. I had no toaster, no microwave, no Internet or home phone. I had no dressers, but I kept my personal things in buckets in my big walk-in closet. So many of the things we think we need are actually just luxuries, and I lived fine without them. The slight inconveniences made me realize just how spoiled I was, since so many people in the world never have soft furniture to relax on and other things we take for granted and consider necessary items. After I moved to State X, I felt like I was that young girl I once was starting out on her own again, though I just turned forty-six; in reflection, it seemed as if God gave me a second chance – a second chance to get it right this time.

Adjusting Once Again
The apartment in State X was about thirty years old and in need of some work, but it was nice. I had lived in apartments

from age 19 to 34, but when I bought my first house, I was so anxious and happy to live in a house where I finally had space and privacy, a yard, a garden, and quietude. After renting a house in Illinois for a year, then living in my own house for the next eleven years, followed by the time in my house in Kentucky for two years, I found it challenging to get used to living in an apartment again where there are a lot of people, noises, and a lack of privacy. I also missed my fenced-in back yard for my two dogs, especially first thing in the morning and just before bed when I would have to walk them, which was an adjustment for us all.

I realized just how spoiled I had become; I thought about this fact especially when I prepared to travel to Kenya for my sixth time to teach at the seminary. Most of my students were incredibly poor, and they would have given their right arms, no, probably both arms, to live in the apartment that I disliked and complained about.

I assumed that the reason I moved to State X was for the job that awaited me. How was this job going to work out? Good? – Yes, as I loved the work from the start. I could not imagine a better job, but it was tough emotionally. Hospital chaplains serve many roles, but one of the toughest roles is probably helping patients and family members deal with crisis and grief that often regards a terminal diagnosis or death. Most importantly, a chaplain needs to love all those he/she serves. Basically, I believe a chaplain needs to care for and love people as Christ commanded.

Chapter Three

Thinking About Dying Alone

One patient who made an impression on me was named Richard. He became my friend and was like a brother. I believe the reason I became a chaplain at a Veterans hospital was for Richard to find true salvation and finally understand Christ's love and the compassion of others so he would not die alone.

Something about this Man

I truly love and care about others, and, of course, all Christians are called to love and care for all people. The apostle Paul wrote, "For the whole Law is fulfilled in one word, in the statement, 'You shall love your neighbor as yourself,'" (Galatians 5:14, from Leviticus 19:18). I loved all my patients with the love of Christ, but there was something unique I was called to do with that love concerning Richard.

Richard came into the MCCU, (Medical Critical Care Unit) and immediately God made me understand there was something about this man... something I was supposed to do, although I did not know exactly what God wanted me to do. He was in great pain, and I had no idea what happened. He was cringing, and as the chaplain I came to see what could be done and to pray for him. He tried to remember a phone number that he attempted to recall, but he kept confusing the numbers. His nurse quietly told me that he may not be fully coherent and reliable, so I wrote down the number for him and left the matter alone for the time being.

The next day, I saw Richard out of critical care and in a regular room. He smiled, as he remembered me. Even when he was in so much pain at our first visit, he smiled when he saw me. I told him that I would visit him regularly, and I did so as time allowed on my daily rounds (which consisted of four wards assigned to me as the chaplain, visiting patients and their families, etc).

Richard had small cell lung cancer, an infection in his heart, blood and lungs, pneumonia, kidney failure, hepatitis B and C, high blood pressure, and diabetes which resulted in a gangrene toe. He had also been a long-time heroin addict, had abused alcohol, and he had unsuccessfully gone through the Twelve-Step program many times. Richard had lived in a mission, though most recently he had been living in a motel. He frequently nodded off while I talked to him and was only coherent part of the time. Despite this problem, I got to know Richard well in a short time, and he invested his trust in me. We developed a good chaplain-to-patient relationship quickly, and we were able to discuss important topics such as the Bible, eternal life, Christian conduct, etc. Richard was a Vietnam veteran who looked about fifteen years younger than he actually was, despite the fact that he had abused himself badly for years. He was extremely kind and was a soft - spoken, polite, quiet man with a warming smile that seemed to melt our souls; even his nurses commented on the nature of his smile.

The infectious disease doctor said that Richard needed to

have his big toe amputated because of the gangrene, but the psychiatrist said that Richard was not competent to make such an important decision. After talking to Richard for a couple of weeks, the infectious disease doctor and I found him to be capable of making the decision about the amputation. Richard understood the consequences of forgoing the surgery – consequences which would cause him to die prematurely. Upon entering the hospital, Richard had misunderstood the doctor and told me that the doctor wanted to "chop off his foot," and he was unsure if he wanted to have such a drastic solution. Once Richard regained a physical equilibrium that allowed his return of near normal mental faculties, and once he realized it was only his toe, and not his entire foot, he decided to have the surgery. With the exception of the psychiatrist, his medical team thought Richard was mentally competent to give his consent, and I received word of his surgery for that next morning. We were all relieved.

The medical team also attempted to contact family members for consent, but there were only two: a brother-in-law and a niece; neither relative ever visited or called him. Richard was entirely estranged from these few remaining relatives, and they no longer had anything to do with him, even to the extent that they could not be located.

Richard informed me that he had no other family, and he only spoke of one friend, Chuck, though I never saw anyone ever visit Richard. The doctors referred to Richard as "socially isolated," and I felt extremely sorry for this man. I prayed with Richard about his surgery and reassured him that losing a toe was better than losing his entire foot, and he agreed. He thanked me for agreeing to see him after surgery.

The next day, he was alert and eating lunch. "Did you have your surgery?" I asked. "No," Richard replied. I asked him why he did not have surgery, and he told me that he did not know.

His nurse was outside of his room, so I asked her; she said Richard was not competent to give the necessary consent in order for the surgery to be performed. I was shocked. As Richard and I were discussing this problem, his infectious disease doctor walked in, and we all agreed that Richard was indeed able to make a competent decision regarding his physical welfare, and we were all convinced that Richard understood to what he was consenting. Being Thursday, the doctor wanted to get the surgery done the following day, since weekends were generally slow and the surgery would have been postponed until Monday; time was of the essence. Thank God – the next day, Richard was wheeled off to surgery, his toe was amputated, and his life was prolonged.

A Monday Morning Visit
On my Monday post-surgery visit, Richard's level of comprehension was vastly improved. Though the adverse effects of Richard's infection were now history, and the danger of his immediate death from the infection were gone, Richard still went through understandable periods of depression, as he knew he was still going to die of cancer. He had taken one round of chemotherapy the previous month (October) which almost killed him, and his chemotherapy was stopped. He also developed an infection in his heart, blood, and lungs and this infection needed to be addressed immediately. Since Richard was much more coherent following the amputation of his toe, we had many good, clear, conversations, and the doctor said that with the infection gone, he would continue to be much more lucid than before. Richard asked if I would see him as often as I could, and I agreed to do so.

Richard had a mustache and the little hair on his head was rather long. He said that before his chemotherapy his hair had been long, and his mustache at one time came down to his chest. Despite his sickness, he was actually still handsome. He had a tattoo, was a Harley rider, and he resembled the typical profile of a biker physically; yet, he was the most gentle and quiet man I knew. He was ashamed of the tattoo on his arm since it had a picture of a skull-faced man, wearing a helmet, and "SS" underneath the bony, death-like face. Richard got the tattoo as a young man, when he was a racist who basically cared nothing for human life. How he had changed, only by the grace and power of God.

His Criminal Past did not Matter
My visits with Richard were good. Because of his extreme isolation, we agreed that he would be the first patient I would visit, and also the last one for the day. In the morning we would talk and read Scripture, and in the late afternoon we would pray. Richard needed a friend and someone he could talk with and trust, and I seemed to be the only person available.

He told me he had been in prison for fourteen years and seven months of a twenty-five year sentence, though he did not tell me the reason. He told me he went to prison again years later (fairly recently) and had served three years on a weapons charge (a convicted felon is not allowed to possess weapons, and he had a gun collection, though he said he did not use them). Being a veteran, it was understandable why Richard liked guns. Presently, I only knew that Richard had committed some violent act, which was hard for me to imagine as I viewed a gentle, soft-spoken man lying limply, unable to walk, dying in a hospital bed.

I Told Him about the Lord
I told Richard about the Lord, and said I wanted to make sure I would see him in Heaven, whichever of us got there first. He gave me that smile... I shared the Gospel with him and we prayed together. Richard told me he had accepted the Lord as his Savior while in prison, through the ministry of the prison chaplains, and was baptized at a Church of Christ where the

inmates were taken who desired baptism. Unfortunately, upon his release from prison, Richard's life fell back into his old pattern, and he fell far away from the Lord. He told me that his criminal past was embarrassing, but I told him that as his friend that his non-Christian and violent past did not matter. Since he had become a Christian, God had forgiven him, and because of His forgiveness, his sins were pardoned – "...as far as the east is from the west..." (Psalm 103:12). I was thankful for his salvation, and also for the ministry of the prison chaplains. With his illnesses, Richard wanted to re-dedicate his life to the Lord.

We always held hands when we prayed, as I did with most of my patients, but he never wanted to let go. He had a habit of taking my hand after prayer and placing it on his forehead. I said to myself, "My dear God, he just wanted a human touch and to know someone cared for him." I understood. Richard looked forward to our morning Scripture reading and our afternoon prayers together. I looked forward to those times as well.

A Good Sense of Humor
Richard always wanted more coffee than the food service gave him, so I would occasionally go to the cafeteria and get him a cup. He said he wanted to "drink with me," then he would laugh, so I told him we would take a trip to the cafeteria and drink a cup of coffee together as soon as his doctors said he was well enough. He said he would actually prefer a glass of Wild Turkey (bourbon) and Diet Coke, but he probably could not get permission from the hospital for the chaplain to take him to the bar down the street to drink! He had a good sense of humor. Richard got excited about the idea of going with me to the cafeteria and finally leaving his room. He had been on contact isolation because of his various infections, so he had been alone for a month, and no one could even come into his room without putting on a hospital gown and gloves. His

infectious disease doctor said it was now safe for him to leave his room, and going to the cafeteria would probably lift his spirits. I told Richard the next morning that I would come back at 2:00 p.m. and take him to the cafeteria. He was happy.

2:00 p.m. came, and I went to Richard's room to find him sweating profusely and quite groggy. I called the nurse to see what was going on with him and I asked her to get him clean pajamas, since his were soaked with sweat and to change his bed linens, and assess his condition. She did those things and said he was fine. Richard insisted on going to the cafeteria. It was not wise, but he wanted to go. In the corner of his room was a walker marked "Physical Therapy," so I assumed Richard had been walking with the physical therapist and was just worn out. He had not gotten out of bed for over a month, so this venture must have been exhausting. Again, I questioned the decision to leave the room for the cafeteria, but since Richard was so insistent, I figured he was up to it. The nurse helped me get him into the wheelchair, and I was uneasily surprised at how light he was. I could have picked him up with one arm!

Off we went to the cafeteria, but when we reached the entrance, they were closing! I asked one of the workers if they would let us in for a cup of coffee, and they gladly said, "Yes." I got two cups, but when we got to the table, Richard began to nod off. He did not look good. He drank two or three sips of the coffee, and I told him we needed to get back to the room and have him checked; he agreed.

When we got to his room, Richard needed to use the bathroom, so I called his nurse. He asked if I would pray with him and see him in the morning, which I did. Again, after the prayer he took my hand and held it to his face as he always did, though for a long time, and I told him I would see him in the morning. Again, I asked the nurse to assess his physical condition, which did not appear good, and I left for the day.

What Scripture Should I Read?
During my drive to work the next morning, I thought about what Scripture I would read to Richard and I was anxious to tell him that I was writing this book you are now reading. I was sure that he would be amazed and surprised. I wanted to tell him that he was the inspiration for the book and that he would be remembered not only by me, but also by everyone who read this book. I knew how special that would make him feel, and I got to work a little early, anxious to tell him. To my horror, when I picked up my list of patients for the day, I did not see his name on his ward, but found him instead on the list in MCCU – the Medical Critical Care Unit!

What happened? Why was Richard no longer in his ward? Why was he in the Intensive Care unit? I immediately went up to the MCC unit and found Richard on a respirator and unresponsive. The nurse said he did not know what happened, and this situation appeared unrelated to any of his other problems. It was too early for the staff to know if he would regain consciousness. I asked if he was going to live, and they said they were unsure. When I went into the room, Richard did not respond to me, but I spoke to him for a few minutes anyway; I held his hand just in case he could feel my presence and I spoke to him in case he could hear me.

The Same Sad Scenario
I visited him later that same morning, and encountered the same sad scenario. I started to think of an old song where some of the lines are, "One more day... one more sunset and I'll be satisfied; but then again... leaves me wishing still for one more day with you." I did not remember the exact lines to the song, but I knew it was about someone wishing for one more day with a loved one, but after that one day, they wanted another and another, etc. I began to cry and quietly sang that song to him. There were things I had wanted to tell him; he could not die yet! Later in the afternoon I visited him again,

and he seemed to respond to my voice, though he still did not open his eyes or speak. I told him about the book I was writing, and I read 1 Corinthians 13, which is what I decided to read that day on my way to work. I prayed. I cried. I told him that I loved him in Christ and that I wanted him to wake up since we had been praying for a miracle of healing each afternoon. I knew he wanted to live, and I asked God over and over for a second chance for one more day!

The medical team assigned to Richard said they would page me if Richard's condition changed – for good or bad. I finally learned Richard had "sepsis" (which is an infection throughout his body which could attack all of his organs). His nurse told me that 80% of people with sepsis die, and with all of the other illnesses that Richard had, this was not looking hopeful. I was frightened and began to tear. I prayed intensely.

One of Richard's doctors and his nurse took my pager number, which also went into his medical file. Richard had no contact person (no family, and no reliable, trusted friend) – how sad. I received a page a few hours later, which made me a little nervous. I was near the MCCU, so I quickly walked over to the unit. The doctor asked about his Living Will or Advanced Directive, which states a person's medical wishes in the event they are unable to speak for themselves at a particular time. I was unsure why his Living Will was not in his room with him in the MCCU, and went to look for it. I told the doctor that I knew he wanted life-sustaining measures taken, since I had previously read his Living Will.

This adverse situation appeared serious and life-threatening and caused me to worry. Going to Richard's former room, I found his belongings, including some books I gave him. Richard was intelligent and loved Shakespeare and Sophocles. I had given him a book on Ancient Philosophy to read and to help pass the time. I left a bookmark in Plato's *Symposium*, which is about love, but when I looked through the book, he had another bookmark in Plato's *Phaedo*, which is about the immortality of the soul. I wondered what he had been thinking. At that point, I really wanted to talk to him, to assure him, and to remove his apparent fear of death.

Earlier that week, before Richard went into the Intensive Care unit, he told me that he did not know whom to name as his Power of Attorney in his Living Will, but he named this friend Chuck, perhaps out of desperation, who also lived in the motel where Richard had last lived, Chuck never even came to visit Richard, and I did not think he was even aware of Richard's desires and last wishes.

Chuck surprisingly called one day while I was visiting, and he was supposed to come and talk to Richard about his Living Will, but he never showed up. Chuck only called Richard a couple more times for the entire three months he was hospitalized, and those times were only to tell him about some particular event. Even though Chuck had a car, he never came to visit Richard. This hurt Richard deeply. Distrusting the steadfastness of Chuck, Richard had previously asked if he could name me as his Power of Attorney, since he said I was his closest "next-of-kin" and the only person he trusted. I agreed to be Richard's Power of Attorney, but we had to agree formally and have the necessary specifications in writing; since this situation was rather atypical, I also had to clear it with my boss. Under the circumstances of Richard being totally alone, after a long discussion, my boss consented to me being Richard's Power of Attorney.

Wishes Regarding His Living Will
Looking through Richard's Living Will again, he wanted to be on life support for all circumstances and to have this directive followed exactly with no variations. We had previously spoken of dying and of Heaven on occasion, and he said there was

always that small area of doubt in his mind concerning eternity. Perhaps Richard's ponderings of eternity grew larger as he filled out his Living Will. Even the social workers with whom I spoke about Richard were surprised at his desire for life support, especially since he was an IV drug user who engaged in such risky behaviors most of his life. Why did he have such a desire to live at this particular and seemingly hopeless point? In my mind, it seemed as though Richard's wishes were motivated by fear, and more than ever, I prayed for him to wake up so we could talk about these issues. Through the help of the Holy Spirit, I wanted to try to help him put those fears aside and assure him that he was forgiven and could have eternal life in Heaven.

In the office with two social workers after Richard suddenly went into MCCU, I was apparently visibly upset, and one of the social workers said she was told by her male colleague that she needed to "toughen up" and not get emotionally attached to her patients. The social worker said she thought doctors and nurses, though they care for their patients, seem to treat them as "objects" to be worked on, almost mechanically, and she never wanted to get to a point of indifference. I agreed with her. I told her that I hope never to "toughen up" according to the definition she discussed, and she agreed.

My Joy as a Chaplain
To cry with my patients and their families and invest myself emotionally and professionally as a chaplain, *is for me* to be Jesus to all the people I meet; actually, that is my *life's* work, not just my day-job, whether I remain a chaplain or not. I MUST love my patients because I represent Jesus to them, and Jesus is love (I John 4:16). When many patients feel they are an object to be worked on or studied by their medical team, a chaplain should work to make each one feel loved and cared for as a human being. Chaplains should give patients a voice while they are in the hospital, and allow them

to be more than patients – to be people who are respected. Loving always hurts in some way, eventually. Jesus chose to love us so much that He died for us. He did not have to take that step of love; but I believe we need the *courage to love*, which means, especially as a chaplain, that hurt will come when patients we have grown to love - die.

Franklin Graham, the man who started the ministry called *Samaritans Purse,* said he wanted his heart to break with the things that broke God's heart. That means that he chose to be in the midst of people who are hurting, and that he too would hurt; yet, he would have the courage to love them, even though such love would indeed hurt. Doesn't death break God's heart? Didn't Jesus cry when he heard Lazarus had died? Should our hearts not break when a death occurs? Isn't that what we do as chaplains? Aren't we called to love those who need love the most, even if that means we hurt when they pass from this earth?

I Cried Sometimes
I went into my office occasionally to cry, and also cried sometimes in the hospital rooms with patients and their families. I grieve with those who grieve; the Bible tells me to do that in Romans 12:15, "Rejoice with those who rejoice, and weep with those who weep." I will always want the courage to love, and I hope God gives that courage to me for the rest of my life, not only as a chaplain, but also in all circumstances. I could still minister to those who look to the chaplain for strength and hope and comfort. I could still love courageously, hurt, cry, and remain sane and strong in the Lord who called us to be like Him and to simply love.

In Henri Nouwen's book, *With Burning Hearts,* he reminded us of the words Jesus recorded in Matthew 5:4, "Blessed are those who mourn; for they shall be comforted." He wrote, "That's the unexpected news; there is a blessing hidden in our grief. Somehow in the midst of our tears, a gift is hidden... Somehow, the cries that well up from our losses belong to our songs of gratitude" (Nouwen, 1997). I have an attitude similar to Nouwen's and have always admired Mother Teresa, as well as Nouwen, who loved the dying. She may have cried with each death, and she loved unconditionally all those for whom she cared. She has always been my role model, and she did not burn out or lose her sanity in her many years of work with dying people in Calcutta.

While I did have to cry on occasion in my office, those times were few, and I was always fine when I got home. I could still function and live life to the fullest because for me, living life to the fullest meant loving all people to the fullest, even when it hurt. What exactly was my role as a chaplain? Could a chaplain's role be different for each chaplain since God made us all unique? Can chaplains deeply love all of their patients? Aren't we called to love all people deeply? Can chaplains be effective in their work and not burn out?

I called several people and emailed a friend in Kenya to pray for Richard, and so the prayers began. My son told me he just finished talking to a Christian woman who asked him if he thought prayers really "worked." My son said that she must not be reading or believing her Bible if she doubts the power of righteous prayers (James 4:2-3). I thought to myself, "OK God... we are praying for Richard, and we KNOW prayer works."

A Page from the Hospital
Jogging on a Saturday morning in a light rain, with my cell phone in my pocket since I was "on-call", I also wanted to be called about a change in Richard's status. I completed half of my usual run when something prompted me to stop and go home. I felt good and wanted to keep going, but that prompting (God) was strong, so I went home. I picked up the pager that

was on the kitchen table and saw a page from the hospital. Was this good news? We had been praying... When I called, the nurse who answered said I had better get to the hospital. My heart sank. I asked if it was bed four (Richard) and she said, "No, it is beds one and two." "How is bed four?" I asked. She said, "We're *coding* right now, so I think you just need to get here." I knew that "coding" meant that *someone stopped breathing,* so I said, "OK," jumped in the shower, dressed and ran out of the house with no idea what to expect. Arriving at the hospital, I went to bed one, who was OK, then bed two, who was also OK; I made sure to pray with both patients and their families before leaving those two beds. I was scared.

I wondered what I was called in for, as there did not seem to be any emergencies. Who was coding? I looked in at Richard, and he was sitting up! His nurse came out and said, "Did you get my call and page?" "Oh, that was you?" I asked. "Yes. Look at your friend. He's breathing on his own... off the ventilator and even speaking." I ran into his room and called his name. He turned and I received the biggest smile I had ever seen! I was delighted (to put it mildly). I immediately began telling Richard how happy I was to see him awake and breathing. He heard what had happened to him, but he did not quite understand everything yet; neither did I, but I was so grateful to that nurse for having remembered to page me. God had given us "one more day!"

Telling Richard about my book, where his history was being recorded, I now had the opportunity to tell him that the he would not only have eternity in Heaven, but his memory would endure on earth with anyone who read my book. I felt as if I needed to tell him everything, since he almost died, and maybe this would be my one and only chance to share about my book with him. Not knowing how long he would live, I was so full of emotions and wanted him to know everything, just in case. He was so surprised and happy. We spoke briefly and held hands. He looked tired so I told him to rest and I would stay with him until he fell asleep. He smiled and squeezed my hand, and said, "OK." When he fell asleep, I slowly withdrew my hand and left the room.

Going to my office, I emailed my friend in Kenya to ask him to keep praying and called my son to tell him the good news, and to keep praying. As I was about to go home, I had another prompting; did I pray with Richard? Oh my goodness (!); in my excitement I forgot. "Well, I can pray with him Monday," I thought. Wait! Remember what my son told me about the woman who asked if prayer works? GO PRAY! The nurses would probably think I was crazy for coming back, but I obeyed, and returned. I walked in and quietly called his name. Richard opened his eyes and looked at me, and I told him I was so excited that I forgot to pray. He smiled and took my hand and I prayed a prayer of thanksgiving, then a prayer for healing. I was obedient and prayed. I saw his nurse as I was leaving and I told him I forgot to pray. He said there are all kinds of ways to pray (of which I acknowledged), but Richard and I prayed together each day, and I felt that need to do so. The nurse smiled and said he would call if there were any changes. I prayed, "God, I am trusting there *will* be changes, and that Richard will be healed." Does prayer work? Yes, of course it does. I just witnessed it, for Heaven's sake, and for the glory of God!

The Second Chance
Did God give Richard a second chance that we prayed for when he went into Intensive Care? I was talking to one of the Christian nurses whom I had gotten to know fairly well, and I told him that I wondered exactly what had happened that day when Richard suddenly went into MCCU. He told me he would look it up in his chart. The nurse was quite surprised to find that Richard was "septic," which is what brought him to the Intensive Car unit. He told me there was no follow-up

when I had asked the nurse to check on him that day when we went for coffee in the cafeteria. When I asked what it specifically meant that Richard was "septic," the nurse told me that his kidneys were not functioning and that he was filled with poison. The poison was in his blood stream which then caused it to be directed to all of his organs, and Richard had stopped breathing that night. The nurse also told me that about 80% of people who are septic die quickly, as their body cannot get rid of the poisons. He was surprised that Richard did not die soon after he coded. Richard was not admitted into Intensive Care until the following morning after he was almost dead. With all of his other health problems, especially the cancer, it was only a miracle that he survived that night. I told the nurse that I had been praying a lot, and the nurse told me it was probably prayer that kept Richard alive. God does hear and answer prayer. God had kept Richard alive, as he should have died that night. Richard was indeed spared and given a second chance.

The next day after church I walked my dogs in a park and enjoyed the beautiful place, as I did every Saturday and Sunday when the weather allowed. Shortly after arriving a phone call came from the hospital that said Richard was released from critical care and changed to a different ward. This change was better since he was moved to a room with three other men to provide him company. Saying a prayer of thanksgiving, I thanked the nurse for the call, and planned to visit Richard after my walk in the park.

Richard was Happy to see Me
Richard was happy to see me. He smiled, and I told him my visit was as a friend and not as his chaplain. He was told that he would always be remembered by me and by those who would read my book about him, and that he would be loved always, even when it hurt. He knew I cared for him and he was always special to me.

We also got on the topic of his former heroin addiction. He told me he had sold the drug in the past, and that he was once a "cold-blooded" man before he accepted salvation through Jesus. Thankfully, Richard no longer used or sold heroin, and he was now a kind and gentle man. I asked him to promise that he would not go back to that life when/if he got out of this hospital. He promised me, but he did not look me in the eye; to me, that was not a sincere promise. Neither of us knew if he would ever get out of the hospital alive, yet my prayer was for that miracle. He needed to strive for something better and to give him hope.

His Living Will
Later that next week, Richard and I met to discuss his Living Will. My boss had previously said that Richard's decision for me to be his Power of Attorney was unusual, but since he had no family or trusted friends except me, that decision was allowed. Richard had checked each box stating that he wanted life support under all circumstances. I asked him why he made such requests. Was he afraid of dying? "No", he said, and then he said something most interesting to me: "No one knows exactly what someone else is feeling when they are unconscious. Maybe I'll feel good."

Richard was a man who just wanted to "feel good," as perhaps he had not felt good for so long (physically, mentally, emotionally or spiritually). He had been treated for depression in the past and treated for heroin addiction and alcohol dependency. He had been married and divorced twice and spent almost eighteen years in prison. He had not felt good in a long time. Maybe he thought he might as well stay alive, under bad physical circumstances, because he might "feel good" for a change. He said that since he thought that no doctor knows with 100% certainty what someone is going through in times of a coma or something serious (where others might withdraw life support), he might finally be happy, so he wished to stay in such a state and remain alive as long as possible. Richard wanted life-sustaining treatments under all circumstances; however, he gave me the authority to determine whether or not life-sustaining treatments should be utilized if he were ever found to be in severe and unmanageable pain yet unable to communicate. I told him that pain could be indicated through body movements, facial expressions, heart rate, and blood pressure, so he told me to use my judgment should the circumstance arise. We finished discussing the Living Will, and Richard reminded me that his life, literally, was in my hands. He said he never trusted anyone, but he knew he could trust me. Little did we know what would take place months later.

The next day, Richard asked me if I would get him a diet Dr. Pepper. The nurse said yes, but they did not have diet Dr. Pepper, though I might be able to get one out of the pop machine. The pop machine did not have diet Dr. Pepper, and being a diabetic whose sugar was not under control, Richard had to have diet soda. Richard did not want a diet Coke, which was all that was available. Promising to pick up a diet Dr. Pepper and return with it tomorrow showed Richard that I could be trusted in small things. By keeping my promise on something small, he could understand that I could be trusted functioning as his power of attorney. Isn't that what God does to us? He tests us in small things to see how faithful we will be in the larger things (Luke 16:10).

Where I Could See God
K., a new social worker at the hospital, though not new to social work, said she was still thinking about the idea of toughening up. I told her to take that idea and throw it right out the window! She laughed, and said that yesterday in church she was thinking and asked where she could see God in the midst of all the pain and suffering and death that we see each day in the hospital. I told her that God is not just

in the beauty that we see in a spectacular sunset or in the beauty of nature. God is not just in the roar of the ocean or in acts of kindness. God is not just in the beautiful, but He is in the broken and the suffering. He is in the broken lives and the broken bodies. Mother Teresa said she saw Jesus in all the faces of the dying people she loved and held, and it was an honor for her to love and to care for them, because she felt she was caring for and loving Jesus Himself. I looked around the hospital; God was everywhere!

Thinking about what kind of hope a chaplain could offer to people like Richard, my thoughts went to other things. Why should he drink that nasty-tasting medicine? Why should he brush his teeth or shave or shower or try to do anything? What motivation can I give him to try? I began to read a book called *Peace, Love and Healing* by Bernie S. Siegel, M.D. Siegel did not advocate so much the power of positive thinking, but he did acknowledge a healing that can take place in the body through hope and optimism. I had to agree. If we can develop heart disease from depression, why not receive healing through love, hope, positive events, and good feelings?

Hoping to be friends with Richard and give him something to motivate him towards recovery... could I give him something to live for with whatever time he had remaining... could I give him a sense of living... could I ensure that he did not merely fade away? Dr. Siegel also mentioned that we could teach people to really live, even if it is just for a short time. Could I show Richard that not only has he given me the courage to love, but also the courage to live – to really live to the fullest? I hoped to teach Richard that people can be trusted, that people can love unconditionally, and that love is everywhere. We can draw close to Jesus, whose body was tortured and abused, when we look at our own broken bodies and realize our need for forgiveness and healing through Christ. Our illnesses are tangible expressions of our need for Christ. Yes, we all die, but miracles *do happen!* Medicine is not the only answer to health, and Jesus is able to do all things.

Praying for Fifteen More Years
We had been praying for fifteen more years of life, which would require a miracle. One morning while praying for fifteen more years for Richard, I heard God ask me "Why?" What would Richard do with fifteen more years if they were granted? I asked Richard, and he said he had no idea. I told him if he were going to ask for more life, he had better realize that life is for others and for God's purpose; our lives are never for ourselves. There was a chance that God would give him more life if he did not utilize it selfishly or destructively. We talked about fifteen more years from the story in the Bible in II Kings 20 about Hezekiah who was told by Isaiah that he was going to die. Hezekiah wept and was depressed with this news, so the Lord gave him fifteen more years. We prayed for fifteen more years each day. Some may disagree and think I was giving false hope to a dying man, but I believe in miracles, and would continue to offer hope to a patient who wants to live, and will continue to give hope to one who wants a second chance. While we knew that everyone must die, we also knew that God is able to heal, though sometimes He does not. Yet, we still hoped, prayed, and made the best use of the remaining time.

Richard was doing much better, though he was still weak and thin. He was six feet tall and down from 175 to 143 pounds. Yet, I knew he was feeling better because he occasionally got in his wheelchair and went down to the first floor, either outside or to the indoor smoke room, for a cigarette. Richard suffered from lung cancer, but he continued to smoke. His smoking angered me, mostly because we had been praying for a miracle of more time, and this habit seemed to contradict his prayers. He knew I would not take him to the smoking area, so he went alone. I let him know I was disappointed and that I refused to take any patients down to smoke, including him. He laughed, though I did not find anything amusing. He was told to take care of himself since he had been praying for healing, but I also knew, fortunately not first hand, the power of an addiction. It was easy to forget that Richard was still an addict. I prayed for deliverance from those deadly addictions.

My refusal to take Richard and other patients to the smoking room slowly changed. When someone knows they are dying and so enjoys smoking, perhaps I should not begrudge their pleasure, even though I could not understand it. Richard's smoking habit was probably what gave him lung cancer in the first place, but I could see that no matter what was said, Richard was going to smoke. Over a short period of time, I began going to the smoke room with Richard almost daily; we talked as he smoked and I half choked.

I Believed in a Miracle
I went to a Christian bookstore over the weekend and bought some Bibles to give to my patients and staff for Christmas; I also bought some anointing oil. In James 5:14-16 it says, "Are any among you sick? They should call for the elders of the church and have them pray over them, anointing them with oil in the name of the Lord. The prayer of faith will save the sick, and the Lord will raise them up; and anyone who has committed sins will be forgiven. Therefore, confess your sins to one another, and pray for one another, so that you may be healed. The prayer of the righteous is powerful and effective."

On Monday morning, I wanted to bring Richard down to the chapel to read James 5:14-16, to confess to one another, and to anoint him with oil for healing. I believed God's Word. Telling Richard about this passage in the Bible, he said he was willing to do this with me. We went to the hospital chapel where it was quiet, and read James 5:14-16; I then said, "We need to do what the Scripture says. Let's first confess to one another any wrong we may have done." Richard confessed a wrong attitude towards some of his roommates, and I confessed a wrong attitude towards some of my co-workers. I then anointed him with the oil, and we prayed together. I believed in a miracle and for James 5:14-16 to come alive.

Reading Richard's chart daily to see the doctor's report on his "multiple health problems," including pneumonia, endocarditis, diabetes, hypertension, hepatitis B and C, acute renal failure and small cell lung cancer was rather discouraging. His chart noted he might be a candidate for Hospice, and he should schedule a palliative care consultation. Palliative care usually means comfort care when there is nothing more that anyone can do for a person through medicine, and that the patient might soon die. My heart skipped a beat and I started choking. It was hard to get my breath. His chart suggested Richard had a short time to live. His medical team was talking about discharging him to the other Veterans hospital almost an hour away, which had long-term care and a Hospice unit. Richard told me his nurse mentioned to him about the medical team having considered moving him to this other hospital, but he did not want to go. He said he wanted to stay near me. Richard had become a dear friend, and I also wanted him to stay. Upset, I went home, got my dogs, sat on the patio, and wrote this non-rhyming, blank verse poem. It is nothing complicated or literary; it just conveys my raw emotions

My Rose

The woods are my favorite place to be.
They are quiet, still and peaceful.
The woods are beautiful.
But tonight I am walking through these woods
And they are still and eerie.
They are so dark. I am uneasy.

Frightened; I feel my heart pounding.
The branches are twisted and broken.
Death lies scattered.
I fall to my knees, crawling,
In search of life, I scream silently.
Ever so silently.
Dead leaves and dead branches
Are underneath me,
Yet in the midst of this deathly darkness
I find a rose.

If I pluck that rose, will it die?
What will happen if I hold it tightly
Against my cheek?
Against my chest?
Will the life be taken,
Or will it grow with my touch?
Touch me, my beautiful rose.
Live. Just simply live.
There is beauty yet to grow.

--Donna Kasik

Shortly after I sat and wrote the poem above, I got a call to go to the hospital, as one of my patients had died. Death is just so awful and so sad... even with our hope of eternal life. Death is the last enemy that God will one day conquer (I Corinthians 15:25-26). God understood and experienced death through His Son Jesus Christ. Jesus experienced the pain of death in his friend Lazarus, and even Jesus wept. That night, I cried at the thought of death.

Chapter Four

Laying Down Our Lives

We need to lay down our lives daily for our friends. We must love others, even when we do not know what is around the corner. We need to love deeply without thinking about what we can get out of the relationship for ourselves. We love because we are commanded to love, and we love for the sake of others.

Biblical Love
Richard and I went to the chapel to pray as we did most mornings. We read John 15 and thought about what it means to lay down your life for your brother. John 15:13 says, "Greater love has no man than this, that he lay down his life for his brother." I used to think that meant jumping in front of someone to take the bullet (a literal laying down of a life for a friend). While I believe it can mean this, especially in the context of Jesus who did literally lay down His life for us, His friends, it can be applicable to other circumstances.

Through the grace and power of God, I have learned to love my patients no matter how they treat me. I have learned to love those who are mentally handicapped, those who yell at me and are angry for who knows what reason. I have learned to love those people who are dying and who I know I will not soon see anymore on this earth. I thought about Richard, whom I had grown to love, though I had no idea where he would be in the near future, or how long he would live. Yet through this experience, I learned to lay down my life for others, on a daily basis, and not necessarily in some dramatic way as Jesus did.

Perhaps the concept of laying our lives down daily was what Jesus had in mind with John 15:13. We love for the sake of love, and never for the sake of what love can give us. I love my patients out of a pure love from Jesus, not because there is anything they can do for me or because I can get anything out of the relationships. What could any of my patients have offered me? What could Richard have done for me? What could I have gotten out of loving him? The pure love of Jesus is why I love. However, I have learned that my patients can teach me so much through their stories, their kindness, their actions, and through their lives. Ministry is ALWAYS reciprocal. Yes, I was in State X as a chaplain, but my patients and their families were there to teach me to love and to live as well.

A quote from Henri Nouwen, in his book *With Burning Hearts*, describes mission work and any type of ministry in the context of always being reciprocal. I learned a great deal from Richard, and we ministered daily to one another. Here is the beautiful quote from Nouwen:

Here we realize that mission is not only to go and tell others about the risen Lord, but also to receive that witness from those to whom we are sent. Often mission is thought exclusively in terms of giving, but true mission is also receiving. If it is true that the Spirit of Jesus blows where it wants, there is no person who cannot give that spirit. In the long run, mission is only possible when it is as much receiving as giving, as much being cared for as caring. We will soon be burned out if we cannot receive the Spirit of the Lord from those to whom we are sent. Each time we reach out, they in turn, whether they are aware or not, will bless us with the Spirit of Jesus and so become our ministers. Without the mutuality of giving and receiving, mission and ministry easily become manipulative and violent. When only one gives and the other receives, the giver will soon become the oppressor and the receivers, victims. But when the giver receives and the receiver gives, the circle of love can grow as wide as the world (Nouwen, 2007).

Not a Typical Sabbath
On one of my Sundays off, as the chaplain on call, the hospital called about an impending death. The leukemia patient was still awake and coherent, though in much pain. I stayed with him and the family for a while, though his sister did *not* want a chaplain present. She was not a Christian and she was also angry and upset. However, the patient was a Christian, so I prayed with him and left the ward. Richard was wheeling himself down the hall, which he did frequently in those days, to go smoke. He had been smoking for fifty years and having an addictive personality surely he would never quit. He somehow denied that the smoking was what gave him lung cancer which was killing him. Richard's denial was surprising.

It was a rough Sunday morning. Awakened by a hospital phone call to visit a patient's room where I was not wanted, was stressful. My sanctuary was the hospital chapel; it was quiet and one could feel the peace of God there. Richard was asked to join me there for prayer and he agreed. After some time to myself, I got some things so we could have the Lord's Supper. Because of my early-morning hospital call, I missed church and felt the need for something normally done at the worship service. The Lord's Supper seemed to be the thing to do. After my time alone and prayer, Richard joined me in the chapel. Richard knew that my coming to the hospital on a day off meant someone was dying or had died. He asked if the person who was dying was OK with the process of death. I told Richard "Yes," and that the patient was ready to die since he was a Christian and knew he would be with the Lord. Richard said, "I wonder how some people can be so comfortable with death?" I asked Richard if he was afraid, and he replied, "Not really," but he said that he did not have peace about it either. I explained how death is not something we were ever meant to experience, and that it was the final enemy for God to defeat, but that we need to be ever ready for it and confident in our salvation.

Richard said he had more of an intellectual knowledge of God, and always had a little bit of doubt. We needed to talk about these fears and doubts, so we read some Scripture together, mostly from the Gospels. We talked about the words of Jesus, what they mean, and the assurance of salvation we can have; if we do not believe completely, then we doubt the truth of Jesus' words. Richard then prayed with me, not only silently as he always did, but I asked him to repeat after me and to pray out loud to God, but only if he wanted to and only if he meant it. He agreed. We prayed for forgiveness and for Jesus to be so real in our lives that we live moment by moment with Him and hear His voice. We prayed for Jesus to live in our hearts and we thanked Him for His sacrifice on the cross. We prayed that if we were the only two people on this earth, that we would know that Jesus would have still come to earth and sacrificed Himself for our sins and that He would still offer us eternal life because He loves us so much and cares about every detail of our lives. We asked for forgiveness and for God to prepare us for the Lord's Supper. I then read John 6 (about Jesus being the Bread of Life) and then Matthew's Gospel and the words of Jesus as He was breaking the bread and drinking the wine with His disciples. We took the Lord's Supper and prayed together.

Richard was told that the concept of life after death was not strange to me, but totally normal and natural. He looked at me in an unusual way. "Look around at nature," I said. "Life dies, and comes back to life all the time. I planted flowers in my yard in Illinois and in Kentucky. I planted perennials. I planted perennials for several reasons; one reason is so I don't have to buy and replant each year, as they come back on their own each spring. Another reason is the mere reminder of life after death. Each winter the flowers die. I pull them up, or cut them back, and they are gone, at least from my eye, but in the Spring, there are more flowers again. They sprout new buds and grow into beautiful flowers. They are the same plant, and the same type of flower, though in a new form. No one that I know finds this to be an unusual or unbelievable phenomenon. The grass dies each winter, but in the spring, there I am cutting it again since it grows like crazy. Nature dies and is re-born; it comes back to life each year. People, who are also a part of nature (remember Adam was made from the dust of the ground) also come back to life as God promised, in the resurrection. Why is that such an unbelievable concept?"

Christmas
My son came from Kentucky to spend Christmas, and I was grateful. This year was the first year I was living not only away from my son, but also away from all of the rest of my family, so it was a bit lonely. Yet, my son took some of my loneliness away, which was wonderful. I was "on call" for the hospital over the weekend and through Christmas. Being on call means that if a patient requests a chaplain, or if there is a death or some type of emergency, the "on call" chaplain must come to the hospital.

At about 9:00 a.m., a good friend from Kentucky called to wish me a Merry Christmas. My son and I were just getting ready to eat breakfast when she called. As we were talking, another call came in. I was afraid that it was the hospital. My friend said she "knew" God would not have me work on Christmas morning, especially with my son visiting. I normally would not switch to another call, but I did in case it was the hospital. The voice on the other end asked, "Is this Chaplain Kasik?" Oh... it *was* the hospital! They told me I needed to come in. I said, "OK," switched back to my friend, and laughed that I was being called into work. As we quickly ate breakfast, I thought I understood God to say that no one knows what He will or will not do, and that He will do whatever He wants to do (Ecclesiastes 7:14). He surely showed us! I quickly finished breakfast and went to the hospital.

Hope in the Midst of Pain
The call was not about Richard, as he was doing much better in those days and constantly left his room, sometimes in his wheelchair, but he usually walked around. Unfortunately, he was always going out to smoke which still upset me. He was weak, but he would hold onto me and practice walking each morning in the chapel when we would go there to read Scripture and pray. Since the chapel was carpeted, he would not slip. His walking was getting much stronger and steadier. The staff was talking about discharging him, but they did not know where he would go since he was previously living alone in a motel in a bad environment that included drugs and prostitution, which he did not want to be around, since he was weak and vulnerable. Also, he would not get the help and support he needed if he lived at the motel. His medical chart recorded that his medical team wanted to move him into a Hospice center somewhere, or in what they called "an institutional center." Who wants to live in that kind of place?

As we sat in the chapel, Richard told me that he might be discharged next week. I asked him where he planned on going, and he said that he did not know. I told him what his chart said. Richard asked, "What is Hospice? Is that like assisted living?" I told him that it was, but for people with six months or less to live. He then began to crack jokes and seemed to remove himself from reality. I began to tear up. He said he was not ready to go lay down somewhere to get ready to die, and that he wanted to live some more and do things and go places. I asked him what he wanted to do and where he wanted to go, and he said, "I don't know... anywhere and anything." He said he wanted to go see a Shakespeare in the Park play when it got warm. Considering the day was December 27 and it would not get warm for months, I wondered if that hope would actually materialize. Then he said he wanted to buy me a brand new Harley Davidson motorcycle with long term financing! We laughed about that, and I told him that was a good idea.

Why can't a dying man, who begins to feel good again, who becomes much stronger than when he first came into the hospital, have some life left to live – even if it is merely watching a play in the park? Is that too much to ask? Richard told me, "When I first came into the hospital, I could not even lift my legs, and now I'm walking! What is this all about? Am I really going to die soon?" Though I knew it was true with all of his illnesses (especially his cancer), it was sometimes still hard to believe, and it was something neither Richard nor I even wanted to believe. I thought, "Sometimes there is nothing wrong with a little denial..."

In my home church back in Kentucky, Pastor Steve talked about the many miracles and healings so many people in other parts of the world talk about and just accept through faith. Miracles are not some huge ordeal for these people, but merely things they expect from God. I wanted to encourage Richard regarding these miracles. From that point on, I refused to tear up, and I encouraged Richard to really live – to live life to the fullest, and to continue to pray for miracles. Richard knew that I would be strong, and he could always lean on me. However, that kind of strength took a lot of help from God, as

I did not possess that manner of strength on my own. Richard told me it was good to have someone to talk with, as he had not really had anyone for years. It seemed that in his past environment many of the people he hung around were not too interested in talking about their feelings, fears, faith, etc., which we all need to do, especially when diagnosed with a terminal disease. It was good to be that person for Richard.

I thoroughly enjoyed conducting the chapel service at the hospital that following Sunday. When the small congregation was invited to come forward, it surprised me to see Richard come up front and kneel at the altar for the Lord's Supper. I mentioned that if they could not come comfortably (due to their physical ailments) I would bring the elements to them. There was Richard, kneeling up front and taking the Lord's Supper. This made me happy and thankful. After the service, we prayed as we did each day, and I anointed him again with oil for a healing.

God Gives New Life
We talked for a while and he told me how much of a changed person he was compared to who he used to be. Richard said that at one point he could care less about human life. Vietnam surely helped foster this harsh attitude. Through desperate attempts at coping with the killing he was commanded to exact in war, Richard had turned to drugs in an attempt to numb the horrors of his past; it is no doubt that drugs also numbed Richard from the compassion he knew prior to war. Having served many years in prison did not help either. Between war and imprisonment, he lost regard for human life altogether and descended into a vicious cycle. Fortunately, by the time we met at the hospital, he had regained his compassion and tenderness through the love of God in Christ Jesus.

While in Vietnam, Richard had come to believe that all people were basically worthless (which was probably a way to cope with having been a gunner) and he therefore did not care much about how he hurt people. How else can one randomly take human life unless one has that attitude drilled into him? But by the time we met, Richard was a kind, gentle, loving, tender-hearted person. He was considerate, patient, and he said he knew that all people are made in the image of God, so there is at least a small spark in everyone which is that God-image. It was surprising to hear him say that, although I should have expected such a remark, especially when I reflected on who he had become. Surely our daily Scripture reading and prayer had helped as well. God works in marvelous ways, or as my dear Kenyan friend Nathan Chesang says, "God is very organized." God moves people exactly where He wants them to be for His purpose, and I firmly believed God moved me to State X for Richard.

Richard came to know the Lord while he was in prison, many years before we met. He went to prison for armed robbery shortly after returning from Vietnam; he had held up a pharmacy for drugs. He shot his gun at the pharmacist, but intentionally missed, since he and his friends had agreed not to hurt or kill anyone. He got hooked on heroin in Vietnam, as many soldiers did, and being trained as a gunner, he developed a love for guns. Is it any wonder when we take eighteen-year-old boys and train them to kill, that they do not return to civilian life the same way? There are no excuses for drug addiction or violent behavior. At the same time, when considering how teenagers once trained for violence, returned with the psychological difficulties that afflict soldiers exposed to violence, what do we expect when they return from war?

There was nothing to do in prison, so Richard picked up a Bible in the cell and began to read, but did not understand what he read. Asking others to help him understand got other guys reading. Each one would take a part and read the stories in the Bible, kind of acting out the pages in skit-form. He laughed, and said it was something to do. Considering that idea, it seemed to make a lot of sense and would surely bring the Bible to life. Perhaps that would be a way to get a group to read the Bible; it sounded like a fun way to learn Scripture.

The prison chaplain helped Richard understand the Scriptures, as he attended the Bible studies in prison. The prison chaplain also baptized Richard at a local church. God lovingly reached Richard with a Bible while he sat in prison with no care for or from people. He had broken the law and hurt others, but God came to his prison cell with His love and mercy.

God hunts us down and pursues us while we are still sinners, because He loves us. In Genesis 18, Abraham kept asking God if He would abstain from destroying Sodom if there were fifty righteous people, and God said that for those fifty He would spare the city. Abraham kept asking God, dwindling down the number until he got to only ten righteous people, and God said He would indeed spare the city for ten. God loves us all, even before we are washed in His blood and changed by the power of the Holy Spirit. Amazing!

New Years Day
New Years Day was time off for me, along with many other non- medical people, including cafeteria workers. Richard had a big appetite and ate breakfast in his room, provided by the hospital's food service. After his first breakfast, he would always get a large second breakfast in the cafeteria. He was so thin, so everyone enjoyed seeing him eat this second breakfast of eggs, sausage, bacon, biscuits and gravy. Knowing the cafeteria would be closed that day, I called him to see how he was doing. He said he wanted a breakfast burrito, which I often made, consisting of a flour tortilla with scrambled eggs, soy sausage, tomatoes, green and red peppers, mushrooms and cheese. Since the cafeteria was closed and knowing Richard was hungry, I brought him another breakfast from

home and we ate together at the hospital. It was nice, and he appreciated it immensely.

In the course of conversation, Richard said he was so skinny that he looked like a Holocaust survivor; he said that several times, because he was about thirty pounds lighter than his normal weight. He also referred to himself as "cancer boy" which bothered me. Remembering that he did have cancer, it amazed me that he could still keep his sense of humor. Not too many people could be jocular under such circumstances. Richard had a good attitude, despite having terminal cancer and being alone in the world.

What does it meant to love someone, even when you do not know if they will live or die, and if there appears to be nothing they can give to you? The idea of "nothing a person can give to you" intrigued me. In the parable of Luke 14, Jesus said that we should invite those who cannot repay us, which of course caused me to think of Richard. Initially, it seemed as if Richard could do nothing for me, but thinking about our developing friendship, he had done a lot for me. While I gave him a pair of reading glasses, some sweatshirts, a coat, some bandanas, and a few minimal material things that he needed, he gave me food for thought and a new perspective on many things. One of those things was his sense of humor. Also, he always wanted to do things for me, like give me quarters to do my laundry, or buy me a juice with breakfast, or whatever came to his mind. How truly wonderful it was just to have a friend to depend on and who could do things for me and I could do things for him. Is that what Jesus meant when He talked about love? I realized that we both did things for each other, and it was not a one-sided relationship. Yes, it was true that he was in the hospital with a terminal illness, but he gave new things to me every day and taught me a lot about life, forgiveness, and love. Learning, caring, and loving people are in the perspective of what people give, and everyone has something to give. Material possessions are the smallest and most insignificant things people can share; life-lessons are the greatest gifts, and these are the gifts that Richard gave to me. Richard gave me more than could ever be repaid; such a notion of love caused me to think about the concept of laying down ones life for a brother. Richard, unless he was miraculously cured from this cancer, would die soon. Was God telling me to lay down my life for my brother Richard, to love him, to help him, and to be a true friend until the end, even though it hurt? At this point, I realized I **must** lay down my life for my brother.

Talking to Richard about his smoking, which seemed to get heavier each day, seemed futile. He had cancer, but we had been hoping for an extension of time and praying for healing each day, yet he was not helping matters by smoking. Yes, I nagged him about it, because I knew those who continued to smoke usually died quicker and complicated their illness. For some reason when we talked about this problem, he abruptly quoted a line from an Edgar Allen Poe poem called *Annabelle Lee*. Some of the lines Richard quoted were:

> *I* was a child and *she* was a child,
> In this kingdom by the sea:
> But we loved with a love that was more than love –
> I and my ANNABEL LEE;
> With a love that the winged seraphs of heaven
> Coveted her and me."

Those lines are truly beautiful. Since I loved the lines of that poem so much, why not write my own Annabelle Lee poem about Richard, whom I had grown to love in my own way; and yes, if you know the full poem – I plagiarized quite a bit!

> I was older, and he was older than me
> At the ward in [...]

> I love him with a love
> That frightens frail love
> Though in strength can part the sea?
> I cling tightly to life
> He grabs at death;
> The demons seem to laugh at me.
> In the darkness of the night
> I cry for the one I love
> Though away, he sleeps peacefully.
> As seraphim gather around my bed
> To wipe my silent tears
> I'll call on Heaven's power
> To comfort his every hour
> Till he realizes what only he can be.
> I live right now and love him,
> As he lives and loves me too,
> With a love as pure as the crystal sea;
> Let the demons fear love's power
> While the seraphim covet
> That power of a love into eternity....

My poem was copied onto a card for Richard. He laughed and said he could not believe how much I plagiarized! We both thought it was funny.

God's Organization

God is organized, protective, and loving. I had been planning to move to Kenya the previous year, prior to my move to the south and this hospital, but at the last minute I was "uninvited," and devastated. I cried for many days over this sudden turn of events. For five years I went to Kenya to teach at a seminary, and each year was asked to consider coming full-time. I declined because I was still in seminary, my son was in college, and I had a house, a mortgage, and a business. But when the time was right, I told the staff that I would surely love to stay in Kenya for a year or so.

After living in Kentucky for almost two years, unable to work on my Doctorate because of financial reasons, and unable to secure decent employment, I thought it was time to go to Kenya. Making arrangements for this move, I told my friends about it and began thinking about raising support money to live there. The seminary had an American branch in California which gave me extensive psychological testing administered by their Human Resource department. I did well psychologically and emotionally, yet, out of no where, an email came from Kenya that basically uninvited me independently of my standing and the decisions in the California branch. Crushed, devastated, and hurt beyond words, I did not understand what happened; neither did Human Resources in California. The California administration was at a loss and could make no sense of this change. However, at the time, there was some reason for this unexpected turn of events, but I did not know what it was. Unsure about going back at all, or if this was God closing the door, I thought the only way to know for certain was to go to Kenya at the end of the year for my two-and-a-half weeks as usual and see if God would show me what to do.

Returning to Kenya soon after they uninvited me, for no apparent reason, I felt peaceful and comfortable with the decision that kept me from moving there. The timing was not right, the seminary administrator who initially invited me was also the administrator who uninvited me; he was the Director and made the final decisions about teaching positions. Seeing him, I felt absolutely no anger or hurt towards him; he was the friend he had always been. We got together several times for tea and dinner, but always with other people, so we did not have the chance to talk privately. He did though agree to a private meeting. Unfortunately, the day of the meeting, he heard that a family member had been killed, and abruptly left the area. Part of me wanted to talk and find out what happened, but the other part thought it was best to leave well enough alone. I was fine with being in Kenya for a few weeks.

After all, I was doing my chaplain Residency which I wanted to do since seminary, and I actually loved my work and returned "home" to continue my Residency for the chaplaincy.

Shortly after leaving Kenya, the news reported heavy fighting, rioting, church burnings, and killings over a controversial Presidential election in Kenya, which included fierce tribal conflict. Many people were fleeing the country and Americans who could not get out were told to stay in their homes because of the violence. There was surely no reason to talk to the Director about my not staying in Kenya for the year. Obviously God was protecting me. It is good to discover God's protection.

When this story was told to Richard, he looked at me somewhat amazed, and then smiled. He asked if I were still planning on moving to Africa. "Yes, in fifteen years. I will be ready at that time to get out of here." Of course, this referred to the fifteen more years of life we prayed for Richard each day. Thinking of Richard and his mortality... what if he became healthy, what kind of life would he live? I still prayed for a miracle, hoping that Richard would discover what a Christian community looks like, especially in comparison to the drug community in which he had lived.

Dreams
Dreaming a strange dream about watching giraffes, that were much larger than normal, walk up a steep mountain... giraffes that gracefully walked into a cloud at the top of the mountain and then disappeared, I wondered where they went. It was as if the earth was flat and they just fell off. Did they fall into an abyss? Did they just fall off the mountain? Did they enter another place? I did not know in my dream and had no way of knowing. Thinking about the dream, it brought me back to Kenya. Twice in Kenya, I enjoyed a safari ride at a game park, but there was a contrast; the beauty of the place and the

cruelty of nature. Watching the animals hunt one another, such as a lioness chasing a wart hog, I was thankful the wart hog surprisingly got away. True, it would have been a meal for a lion family, but I did not want to see the kill. A short while later we were forced by our driver to watch water buffalo fight to the point of death for about thirty minutes. What entranced me was watching the giraffes in the background. Beyond the fighting and attempts at death, I watched many giraffes slowly, gracefully, gently walk by in the background. Those tall, graceful creatures were so beautiful.

Perhaps my dream had something to do with all of the fighting going on in Kenya, from which God spared me, and the beauty that still exists in life and in the people all around us. Perhaps the dream was also about the beauty we can see in the midst of illness and death, when we look past what is right in front of us, to the heart and soul of the dying people; when, like Mother Teresa, we see Jesus in the faces of the sick. I wanted to pass such beauty along to Richard, especially since he had fought depression most of his life.

It is sometimes hard for me to imagine that I can think life is so beautiful right now, when for so many years I thought of life as a slow, painful, lonely struggle. Having had death all around me at the hospital, and considering Richard's terminal cancer, somehow I saw so much beauty in life. I saw so much beauty in people all around me – even in those suffering intense physical illness. Perhaps it was because I began to see Jesus in our suffering. Perhaps it is because now I watch the giraffes, rather than the water buffalo.

God and Suffering
I read a book written by David G. Benner entitled, *Care of Souls: Revisioning Christian Nurture and Counsel.* In this book the author wrote, "God is somehow particularly present in those who suffer." He also wrote that, "If we rightly understand the

revelation of the cross, we will understand that it is within suffering – our own and that of others – that Christ reveals himself... Only when we stand with those who suffer pain, humiliation, starvation, and poverty and look at the world through their experience will we truly know the God who came into the world to share human pain. Openness to suffering is really openness to life. Suffering is an inevitable part of life, and if we are open to any of life, we must be open to it all. If we run from pain in ourselves and others, we will never know peace or joy with any real depth" (Benner, 1965). It is this beauty I saw in the giraffes, amongst the suffering, pain and death, both in Kenya and in my dream, (and later, in Richard) though I did not know where that beauty led in the dream. Perhaps it does lead to suffering, but we can experience God in the midst of it all. As Mother Teresa said, she saw Jesus in the faces of all those who were suffering and dying, and she felt honored to care for them because of that reality. I felt the same with my patients and, of course, mostly with Richard.

Richard's Old Life
Richard was given a four-hour day pass to leave the hospital. It was Saturday, so I told him I would pick him up. He wanted to go back to the motel where he was living and check on his car, his mail, and he wanted to see if he had any material possessions left. Since he had been in the hospital for two months, he was unable to pay his rent. His friend Chuck called one day to inform Richard that everything he owned was stolen. Richard lived in a motel where one pays by the week, so he believed the owner stole all of his things, since the owner was a drug addict and a crook.

Richard came outside shortly after I pulled up to the hospital. It was convenient for him, as it was a short walk from the elevator. He looked so skinny. He got in the van and off we went. It was so good just to see him walking and getting in and out of the van, and it was also good to see him in clothes, rather than in hospital pajamas. When he first arrived at the hospital it was uncertain if anyone would ever see him walk. I asked where he needed to go, and he told me that he needed to go to the motel where he had been living.

The motel was full of down-and-out people who appeared to be drug addicts and alcoholics. People seek their own. I saw many broken people as I waited in the van while Richard took care of some business. The first thing he did was look at his car, which his closest "friend" Chuck had wrecked and tore up the clutch. The car could not be driven any more, but Richard was not even angry; as usual, he took all things in stride. Richard had forgotten his car keys, and the car was locked, but he looked inside to find his DVD player gone. The car was locked with no evidence of a break in. Richard told me that Chuck was a junkie and probably had pawned the DVD player for drug money.

Richard went to Chuck's room, but he was not there. A woman came out and walked Richard back to my van. She smiled and waved to me, and I later learned she was sharing a room with his friend Chuck who had both cancer and AIDS. She looked badly abused by drugs, which proved to be an accurate assessment. She was a crack addict. She told Richard that since he was not there to pay the rent, the owner of the motel threw all of his things out, after taking for himself whatever he wanted, and then the people who lived in the motel came and took what they wanted. Richard no longer had any material possessions. Again, he seemed to take it all in stride. He hugged her, and he got in my van. She told Richard she "loved" him and that she would see him when he got out of the hospital. I was sorry about Richard's belongings. He said, "Well, my stuff just went the way of all things," which he said often. His attitude makes me think of Hebrews 10:34 which says, "For you showed sympathy to the prisoners, *and accepted joyfully the seizure of your property, knowing that you have for yourselves a better possession and an abiding one"* (italics mine).

What amazed me was that Richard's friends and the motel owner knew he was in the hospital since Chuck was the one who found him unresponsive in his room and called the ambulance. Yet his possessions were still thrown out, and even his friends did not ask if they could get them and keep them for him. When I mentioned that to Richard, he said they would have sold or pawned his things anyway as well, as they were all drug addicts; the game they all played there was ripping one another off, sort of taking turns doing so. What a terrible way to live! I said, "That is not a game I would want to play!" Richard agreed, though I knew that he might have done such things himself for many years as a heroin addict.

What a different world Christ offers us, in contrast to the terrible and depressing world at the motel. Had this environment been a Christian community, his belongings first of all would not have been thrown outside, but would have been left in a safe place for him to get when he returned. If there were any people in a Christian community who had some extra money, his room would have been paid for as well and left just as it was for him to come back, if he so desired. I thought about the apostle Paul who told the owner of the runaway slave in the book of Philemon, to charge the apostle with whatever Philemon's slave owed him, and Paul himself took care of the bill. Also, in the story of the Good Samaritan (Luke 10), the Good Samaritan offered to pay the innkeeper to take care of the stranger whom he helped. Had this thought even occurred to Richard? I did not want to belabor the point at that time, since he was hurt. It is baffling to consider the contrast between the Christian life and communities run by Satan, and to see so many people still reject Christ.

Several times when Richard's sugar bottomed out (he was a

diabetic) and he was passed out, unresponsive, and almost dead, his "friends" found him – and instead of getting some sugar into him as his friend Chuck normally did, the others would go through his pockets, take his wallet out, steal his money and whatever else they could get. Chuck told me about this awful scenario one day; it is one of the sickest and most disturbing things I have ever heard in my life. It is absolutely detestable.

What many Christians forget when saying, "There, but for the grace of God go I," is the poignant truth of that saying. Who knows what happened along the way in life that made some people so broken. How did some get so lost? Why is this man such a bad alcoholic, or that woman a prostitute, or those people drug addicts? What were they looking for that they never received? What kind of families did they come from, and what values or lack of values were handed down and taught or modeled? Was self-respect ever an option? Did anyone ever love or care for them, and did they even know how to love? So many of us grew up in stable middle-class families, went to Sunday School, had parents who loved us and were involved in our lives as children, and we think all children grow up this way and learn the values that we learned.

Maybe that prostitute was sexually abused, and the beauty and purity of proper sexual intimacy within marriage, respect of the body, and personal modesty were never a remote thought. Maybe that drug addict grew up with addicted parents, and the drug lifestyle was considered normal. Maybe that veteran could not deal with the killings and horrors he experienced and participated in during war, and he turned to alcohol and drugs to numb his pain because he never had anyone to help him through his struggles. I learned one thing through so much sadness and struggle: we cannot be so quick to judge the brokenness in others, especially when we are all broken before Christ. Thanks to God that He can repair our brokenness; how much more do we need to make this fact known to those who are so far from our Savior?

After we left the motel, we took a short walk in the park, which was close to the hospital and one of my favorite places. We sat on a bench and talked about the day's events. We talked about his friends and how Christians would (or at least should) treat one another so much differently. He was in agreement. We shared about how some people are slaves to something, whether it is drugs, alcohol, sex, money or whatever, and in II Peter 2:19, Peter wrote, "...for people are slaves to whatever masters them." Paul often used the theme of the slave and master relationship in his Epistles and it is written that we should be slaves to Christ, who should master our lives. Paul often called himself a "bondservant" or "slave" to Christ Jesus. Richard agreed, and said, "Without Christ, there is *nothing*." He was starting to get it.

The events at the motel and the brokenness in so many people saddened me. Jeremiah 1:5 says, "Before I formed you in the womb I knew you, and before you were born I consecrated you." God planned a life for each one of us before we were born, and surely it was not the life of those drug addicts and alcoholics living in the motel, who stole from one another. They missed the purpose of their lives, and settled for so much less than what could have been. Such reduced life-styles are pathetically sad.

At age sixty Richard said he had a lot of regrets, because most of his life was wasted. He was a heroin-addict, drank a lot, spent years in prison, and hurt people. He knew that he missed out on his purpose in life. Richard only wanted to live before he died, and who could possibly blame him? I said, "Well, at least you know you will live in eternity." "Yes," Richard said, "but there is a lot of life here on this earth too that I missed out"; that's true... and we can never get that back. He smiled, squeezed my hand, and gave me a hug. The main reason I prayed for fifteen more years of life for Richard was so he could have that chance.

Turning my back on Richard now was not an option, especially since he had come so far spiritually and emotionally. Richard said that I represented what a Christian should be, for love and sacrifice are what makes a Christian. After all, doesn't Scripture say that love is laying down one's life for a brother? (John 15:13). Isn't a friend supposed to be there for another until the end? Or was I supposed to bail out in cowardice when the pain got too tough on me? Was I to leave him to suffer with his cancer and to die alone? No, I could not do that! If I represented Christianity to Richard, there was no choice but to love him and do all I could in whatever form that would take. That was the least I could do.

Never too late to Love
Richard depended on me for many things, and he needed the love of a friend. I could not leave him alone, since most of his life had been spent alone, even if it was his own fault. His past just did not matter anymore. What did matter is that he saw what Christian love was, and in Christ, our love is always sacrificial; after all, look at our role model – Jesus – who willingly suffered and died for us.

Thinking about Richard and how he wanted to live as fully as possible before his earthly end, I thought of my own life. None of us have any idea when we will die; anything could happen at any time. For me, living life to the fullest means loving all of God's creation to the fullest, and loving deeply always involves pain, eventually. The only way to avoid pain in life is to avoid loving relationships. 1 Corinthians 13 came to mind. Especially the translation from the Ancient Eastern text of the Peshitta;

"**Love is long suffering** and kind; love does not envy; love does not make a vain display of itself, and does not boast, does not behave itself unseemly, **seeks not its own,** is not easily provoked, thinks no evil; rejoices not over iniquity, but rejoices in the truth; **bears all things, believes all things, hopes all things, endures all things. Love never fails**" (the bold letters are my own addition). Jesus never said love was easy.

Richard was to be released from the hospital on January 11, after almost three months of recuperation. We discussed his options as to where he could go; he did not want to go back to the motel or be alone in an institutional Hospice center. Richard had no family and was too weak because of his numerous health problems to survive on his own for long. He collected a small disability check. I asked him what he needed, and he said, "Everything." I decide to take Richard to my home.

Chapter Five

Thinking About a Terminal Diagnosis

I loved my dog, Millie, that cute, little goofy dog that I had for only a few months. And I loved Richard who had a thirst for life in spite of a terminal diagnosis that was taking him away, despite my prayers and loving care for his illness. Richard, too, was in my life for only a few months.

My Dogs
Both of my dogs were rescue dogs obtained from the farm in Kentucky. The veterinarian said my dogs were sick but treatable; he gave me some medicine, and that was about it. Millie, the smaller, younger dog that I had owned for only four months, also had an ear infection which did not surprise me since the other dog, Pebbles, also had those same problems. I had obtained both of these dogs from outside living conditions where such afflictions are common and can linger. Millie was dropped off by someone and left at the front gate. There was no history on her and she continued to get worse with each day. Millie became more and more lethargic. I took her back to the vet, and he gave me some other ear medicine and some antibiotics. The vet did not know what was wrong with her. The next day, she became even worse.

The vet told me he thought Millie had a brain tumor, and may need brain surgery. These medical tests were getting way beyond my financial abilities.

Pebbles recovered, but Millie continued to decline and would surely die. I told Richard that I did not want Millie to die in my apartment as there was no place to bury her. I wanted to go back to my home in Kentucky so she could be buried behind the garage. The occasion was also used to show Richard my home.

Richard kept saying that perhaps she would not die and would indeed get better. We were hoping for that, but I knew Richard was thinking in terms of himself when discussing Millie's recovery. Soon after we got to my house in Kentucky, Millie's health changed, and during the night she began writhing and foaming at the mouth. The following morning the vet said she needed to be "put down" and I cried. Richard was most considerate of my feelings and took care of the procedure himself, sparing me the pain. I left the room, and within minutes, Richard walked out with a small cardboard coffin, which he and my son buried behind the garage. I loved that cute, goofy, little dog that I had for only a few months.

My Fears
Richard, Pebbles, and I returned to the apartment after a few days in Kentucky. I bought a couch and a nice, soft, comfortable chair for Richard to enjoy. A few days later, Richard looked terrible, and he and Pebbles both became extremely ill. It appeared that everything and everyone in my house was going to die except me, and I was devastated! Arriving at work, I locked my office door and began to sob. There was just too much death staring me in the face.

Richard was feeling "pretty rough," as he sometimes said. He said he thought he was going to die the previous night and again in the afternoon. Was he so scared that he wanted me to stay home? Did he really feel that bad? I knew he looked bad... I began to sob. Then we prayed and embraced and suddenly, I had a peace come over me and knew that he was not going anywhere, and I said, "Richard, I don't think you are just suddenly going to die. You'll have your good days and your bad days. But you'll be here when I get home, and I'll get home early." He was scared, and said, "I'll be watching you from above." We both cried for several minutes, but then I felt God strengthen me and I understood that things would be alright for now. Before I left for work, I made sure to tell him that I would see him shortly. He smiled. He then said, "Ya, I guess I'm not just going to suddenly die. I think I'll just kind of fade away."

Drug Abuse
Richard no longer used heroin (which I would never have allowed in my home), but he used his medicinal morphine in the same manner, and I found this to be totally unacceptable and abusive. I had spoken with Richard over and over about his IV morphine use, which nauseated me because it is not supposed to be used that way, but he would not stop.

He went to church with me each Sunday, but we often left the service early because he would nod-off on account of his morphine abuse. He was still prone to infection, which worried me. Whenever a needle is inserted into a vein, there is a risk, no matter how slight, for infection. The biggest obstacle to our friendship and our shared living arrangement was the grossness of my discovering that Richard tied his arm up and stuck a needle into it, which was contrary to the design of Richard's oral morphine prescription.

Richard always tried to hide this habit from me. He did not think I knew what he was doing when he went into the bathroom to inject his morphine. I knew people from the past who were IV drug users, which is a habit that had always sickened me. The fact that he was in the bathroom for so long and the strange noises I heard made me curious. My apartment had two doors into the bathroom, and the first time I saw him shoot up was when I went into the walk-in closet which leads to the sink-area of the bathroom, and the other bathroom door was open where I saw him injecting his morphine. It was a sight that repulsed me. I cried and asked him what he was doing and why. He was angry that I saw him do this, but he said that he just began doing that with his morphine and that it was a more effective way to relive his pain. He thought I would understand, and that I should be supportive of him, since I should want to see his pain relieved in the quickest possible manner. After all, he was dying anyway. What convoluted and disturbed logic! I told him I could not deal with this practice and it was not allowed in my home. I soon learned, through his friend Chuck, that this was a habit that Richard had done almost all of his life, especially in the past with the heroin, although Richard told me he often "ate" the heroin and did not always shoot it.

Tough Love
Because of Richard's self-destructive practices, I kicked him out of my home, and returned him to the motel where he used to stay. I told him that if he wanted to live in his self-defeating way, then he was more than welcome to do so in his former, dangerous environment. He was not allowed to live as a junkie in my home. Boundaries had to be placed somewhere. Even though he was dying, I could not let him live however he wanted to live with a habit I found reprehensible. At the same time, I found difficulty with my stance, as I wondered how much "tough love" should be given to a dying person. Should I give any "tough love," or was I too harsh on a dying man? Yet, I had to maintain my sanity, and I was beginning to get chest pains, high blood pressure, and headaches, all as a result of this stress.

Thinking About a Terminal Diagnosis

After a day or two I would feel sorry for him and he would tell me that he would stop shooting his morphine. He told me that he much preferred to live at my place and that he could not imagine living anywhere else. He soon moved back in to my home, and I took care of him. We both knew that he would die shortly on his own if he continued with his habit, and neither of us wanted that to happen.

Richard would abstain for a day or so, but then he would be right back at his habit again. It seemed that Richard did not know how to live without his drug use, and I did not and would not live with it, though we cared for each other in spite of it and wanted to stay together. This issue though soon came to a head one February morning.

The 911 Call

Early Sunday morning when I was asleep in my bed I heard a strange noise coming from the living room... a moaning-type of sound. Listening for a few minutes, I continued to wake up trying to figure out what the noise was. Finally in the living room I found Richard on the couch barely breathing, gasping, and in convulsions. He was unconscious, so I called 911 and the operator told me what to do until the paramedics arrived. Soon, the small apartment was filled with paramedics who finally got an IV into his hand. It was a frightening, violent scene. For some reason the paramedics could not take Richard to the Veterans hospital so they took him to another hospital, and told me to follow.

Arriving at the emergency room, I found Richard sedated, but unconscious. Blood was all over the floor and his clothes were ripped to shreds. Apparently, his convulsions had escalated. There was a policeman outside of his door, which I attributed to them having looked at his veins and having discovered the vial of morphine he carried on his belt along with the metal measuring spoon which was in his pants pockets. The medical staff did not have his full medical history as the Veterans hospital did, but the doctors could put two and two together.

Richard's condition was serious and the doctors told me they needed his Living Will for life support issues. Retrieving a copy from my office, I brought it to the hospital, and asked if he was going to die. The doctors said they did not know.

Once Richard was stable, they transferred him to the Veterans' hospital and put him in the Medical Critical Care unit, which is the unit where I first met Richard months before. The doctors had no idea what happened or what was wrong with him, and they had many questions. I told them how I found him and that the night before he had complained of a headache and neck-pain, which was unusual. They thought he might have meningitis and they asked my permission to administer a spinal tap, which came out negative. I told the doctors about his morphine abuse. It appeared he had overdone his self-medication, which seemed to be a reasonable assumption that accounted for the present circumstance, which almost killed him. He remained on a ventilator and unconscious for the next two days; the doctors and nurses were unsure whether he would live or die. Again, I was asked for his Living Will.

An Apparent Conflict of Interest
Because Richard and I were friends, and he was literally dying, I was told I could not visit him during working hours nor have access to his medical chart anymore, since the situation was an apparent conflict of interest. My boss came into my office to speak to me. He told me that I would need to separate my work from my personal life, and that I would be fired if I did not. I agreed that I could make such a separation. I visited Richard before work, on my lunch break, and after work and prayed for him to wake up and live.

Once Richard was awake on the third day, his oncologist asked him if he knew why he was there, and Richard said, "Yes... I was told by Donna that I overdosed on morphine." The doctor thanked him for being honest, "as he had always been," and the doctor told him that he did not have long to live because of his cancer. In a somewhat matter of fact manner, the doctor told him he was lucky to be alive at the moment. We were both in tears. I said, "Richard, I cannot take you home with this type of abuse and behavior." A tear ran down his cheek. I then said out loud, "Oh God, what should I do?" His nurse, whom I had not met before, kept walking in and out of the room. She finally said to me, "I hesitate to say this to you since I am a nurse and you are the chaplain, but I heard what you said and I prayed about it and God clearly impressed me that you should take him home. God will give you the strength to care for him, and you will regret when something happens to him if you don't take care of him." I was shocked. Does God answer prayer that quickly? I looked at her and said, "I might need confirmation on that decision."

Seeking Godly Counsel
Calling my pastor in Kentucky, he was asked what he thought, since he was greatly respected as a pastor and as a person. He told me that I needed to be careful of my emotions, as this situation was surely a painful one. I told him that the emotional aspect was too late since Richard and I were close friends who already loved each other. My pastor said that love is always a good thing. Pastor Steve told me I needed to be concerned with my Christian witness. I knew he was referring to me having a man live with me who was not my husband, though he knew Richard and I had not been, nor would be living a married life. However, it might not look good to those on the outside. I told him that no one knew me in this area, and that no one knew whether I was married or single, Christian or otherwise, so that issue did not seem to be a factor in this decision. I also called some trusted Christian

friends, and they all told me it would be a Christian act of love to take care of him until his death and that they would be proud of me if I did so. I knew this was what I should do, and felt confident that Richard was the reason I came to this state and to this particular hospital.

Richard was told that he would go to my home when released, but things would have to change: there would be neither syringes nor morphine for self-medication; these would remain in my possession and would be administered by me as needed. Ordinarily his blood sugar level and blood pressure was checked by me periodically throughout the day, so this measure would just be one more medical step for me to take. Richard was told that he was going to be released the next day, and he agreed to this arrangement. All the metal spoons in the house were replaced with plastic. The syringes and morphine were placed in a lock-box in my locked car (Richard did not have keys to my car). This change was required for me to care for him. He reluctantly agreed.

Medical Council
The doctor and the woman in charge of Hospice/Palliative Care came to talk to me the day before he was to be discharged; they basically told me that I was crazy for even thinking of taking him into my home, and that he should go to the Hospice center that was so far away from my apartment where it would be difficult for me to see him. I told them that Richard did not want to go there, because he would be alone. The doctor and the head of palliative care were both angry with me. They told me that since he had abused himself all of his life, he did not need this kind of special care, and that if I took him home I "would not have a social life." I could not believe that my social life would even be a thought under such circumstances! My social life was not my priority at this time.

They then took me into a conference room to tell me what a mistake I was making and that because of his drug abuse my life would be in danger. I laughed and said they had to be kidding, since Richard was a kind, gentle man who would not hurt a fly; besides, he was weak and could not hurt me even if he wanted. I knew Richard would never consider hurting me anyway, and since he had become a Christian, he did not want to hurt anyone. Then the doctor told me he should be a DNR (Do Not Resuscitate), though he had a Living Will that stated that he did not want to be a DNR, but that he wanted to live at all costs. He had always said, "Bring me back if I go!" I realize most terminally ill people are indeed DNR, but had Richard had that status, he would already have been dead either from the time he was intubated from the sepsis several months back, or in the overdose situation, as he was again placed on life-support and survived.

Richard was only sixty-years-old and he was not ready to die. He said that there were still things he wanted to do – simple things like going to the park, the art museum, out to eat, anything... and to spend time with me, his friend. I would not deny him those things. He wanted to get out and drive and go to the store, since he loved to shop; when I told them about his wishes, they laughed and said he would never do any of those things. I told them they were wrong. Then, the most surprising thing was said. The doctor said, "Well, let's just say that he is not competent to make these decisions... let's make him a DNR and put him in Hospice care." I was shocked, and I told them that his mind was quite clear and capable of making decisions, though they disputed me because of his drug use. Richard was an intelligent man, who at that moment knew exactly what was going on. He was getting agitated and said to me, "I want to get out of this hospital. If I'm going to die soon I want to get out and live!" I told him that he would be discharged the next day. I went home to get ready, once again, for Richard.

I called Richard in the evening to see how he was doing, and he suddenly panicked. He said a nurse just came in and placed a red band on his arm, and he wondered what that meant. "It means they made you a DNR, which you are not to be," I told him. I asked to talk to his nurse, who then cut the band off as I was speaking to her. I told her that I would talk to the doctor the next day. When I got to work that morning, one of his nurses ran over to me and asked if I knew what was taking place. "What do you mean?" I asked. She said his doctor took him off all medications, including insulin. Richard still ate three big meals a day plus snacks, so without insulin, his blood sugar would become sky-high. One of the nurses said that he would simply go into a diabetic coma and die painlessly within a couple of days. Again – utter disbelief and shock! "He's not going to do all those things he wants to do anyway," she said. I was amazed, and asked, "Why don't I just take a gun and blow his head off? It would be the same thing." Another nurse nodded her head and said that she agreed with me. I asked for the charge nurse and told her to call his doctor immediately in order to put him back on all medications. She got the doctor on the phone, within minutes, who said we must have had a misunderstanding. As far as I was concerned, there was no misunderstanding, just unethical cruelty and negligence.

The doctor placed Richard back on all medications. The palliative care woman asked me why I had insisted. She told me that poking his finger to check his sugar level with his glucometer and giving shots of insulin was "invasive" and would be too much trouble for me to do, so I should just forget about it. I was horrified at what I heard. I told the doctor that good palliative care (otherwise known as comfort care) does not involve just keeping a person comfortable physically, but it also incorporates mental, spiritual, and emotional well-being. If I told Richard that we were not going to check his sugar anymore or give him insulin, especially with the amount of food he still ate, he would go into a complete panic – *that is not good palliative care*. I also told both of those women that I knew Hospice did not discontinue insulin. Furthermore, I also knew that when a dying person no longer ate, then, at the discretion of the patient or family (if the patient was not competent or conscious), insulin could be discontinued. What was happening, in my opinion, was nothing more than getting rid of "one of the least of these" who was viewed as being too much trouble. Did they not see that Richard was a person made in the image of God (Genesis 1:27) whom God loves? Did they not know that Jesus said when you take care of the sick, or visit those in prison, or give a cup of cold water to the least of these, you are doing it unto Him? When we do not do any of these things for the "least of these," we are neglecting Jesus. I do not want Jesus to say to me, when I see Him face to face, "Why didn't you take care of Me?" (Matthew 25:34-46).

The Desire for Life
Richard was so anxious get out of the hospital. He started to get agitated, and before I knew for sure if he was to be discharged he asked for his clothes and began to get dressed. I told him to hang on and to let me see what was happening concerning his discharge orders, but he said, "If I'm going to die I want to get out of this hospital." The nurse came in shortly after that and said he was ready to go. I brought the car around, got a wheel chair and took him home. It was a Thursday afternoon, and I told him that I would take Friday off and be home with him over the weekend to help him as he needed. He was happy. Thursday, Friday, Saturday, and Sunday came without incident. Richard did not shoot his morphine and he did not bother me about it either. He never became angry, violent, or hostile as everyone told me he would when he wanted his drugs. Life seemed to finally be a little "normal," all things considered.

Not having the mind of an addict, a big mistake was made at bedtime Sunday night after an uneventful weekend. I placed two morphine tablets on his nightstand and told him that some morphine was available if he experienced any pain during the night. He thanked me and went to bed. The next morning I saw that the morphine was gone and asked if he had taken them during the night. He told me he had. Richard had a medical appointment at the hospital Monday morning. He always rode with me to work on the days of his appointments and just got there a little early. I would take him home when his appointment was over and use that time as my lunch break. However, this particular day he said the appointment time was too late in the morning and that he did not want to wait around for so long. He assured me that he would be fine to drive himself, though I did not think that was a good idea. I worried about Richard driving, but he said he would be alright. I reluctantly agreed; after all, he was a grown man and could make his own decisions.

Later that morning I went down to the area where he had his appointment, but I did not find him. I went to the cafeteria to see if he stopped for something to eat, but he was not there. I went over to the hospital store where he shopped – not there. I went to all the places I knew he would go to smoke – not there. I called him – no answer. I went back to where he was supposed to be for his appointment, and the receptionist said he never came. I panicked. I called his cell phone again, and he finally answered. "Richard, where are you?" He replied, "I'm at home; I was 'sleep." He sounded incoherent. I kept repeating, "Richard, where are you? Why aren't you here at the hospital?" He replied, over and over, "I was 'sleep." I had no idea where he was since I called his cell phone. I thought perhaps he went to the motel for drugs. He sounded like a mess. I had no idea what was going on or where he was, but I thought I had better get home immediately, for something was surely wrong. I went out to the parking lot where he would normally park, just in case he was there, but he was not. I ran to my car and hurried home, and I talked to him on the phone the entire time I drove home; I dared not hang up.

The blinds were closed at the apartment, which was strange since they were never closed during the day. I put my key in the lock, turned the door-handle, but could not get in since the chain-lock was fastened. I was worried sick, and I was furious at the same time. I wondered what was going on inside the apartment. I heard Richard, but I could not see him or get to him. We continued to talk to one another on the phone. I began yelling and pounding on the door until I finally saw him come over and unlock the chain. Richard was still talking incoherently to me on the phone, even though we were face to face, until I grabbed the phone out of his hand and asked what was going on. He looked strange. I immediately checked his blood sugar, which I could tell was too low. While his sugar-level was indeed very low due to his diabetes, it would have explained some of his bizarre behavior, but it did not explain the locked-up house and the drawn blinds. My heart sank. I had told Richard in the past that his IV drug use not only disgusted me and was a habit I refused to accommodate, but also, since we were in an apartment, when there was work to be done or building inspections, that after a couple of knocks the maintenance workers might just walk in since they had keys. If they saw him shooting up, we would be tossed out of the apartment. I thought about this scenario... could Richard have gone back to this habit already? I checked his blood sugar, and it was very low. I got some orange juice and some yogurt in him, and made him some lunch in order to bring his sugar up. I still needed to determine whether or not his blood-sugar was the only reason for this strange behavior, though I knew in my heart that there was something else going on as well.

Next, I needed to figure out why he missed his doctor appointment. I noticed that Richard's black leather jacket was hanging over the kitchen chair, and I picked it up. Inside one of the pockets was a small bag of syringes in a Walgreen's bag, and in the other pocket was a set of metal measuring spoons. I then found the plastic outer wrap of a cigarette pack with what looked like a morphine pill inside of it. "Where did you get the drugs Richard?" I assumed it was morphine, but in my anger at the time, I was still unsure. I was furious. My first day back to work and our newly agreed arrangement was already failing. I guess it was true: Richard would never give up his needle addiction. He was still coming around from his low sugar level so he was not 100% himself while I went through his pockets, otherwise this would have been a bit of a verbal struggle; Richard though, was always gentle and non-violent.

I called his friend Chuck to ask if he had been out to the motel to get drugs, and his girlfriend Julie answered and told me, "No, he has not been here," while she cried and insisted she and Chuck never have and never would give him drugs. Richard kept telling me that I gave him the drugs, but how? He repeated that over and over, and finally he told me those were the pills I left on the nightstand for him the night before. He said he did not need them during the night, and thought he would save them until I left; he then went to the store for needles and metal spoons. How could I have been so ignorant?

After Richard had some food, he finally started to get back to himself and become coherent. I told Richard he had two choices: 1) He could pack his bags and move to the motel and be gone before I came back home from work, or 2) he could look up phone numbers for Narcotics Anonymous and start going to meetings again. I was furious. I slammed the door and went back to work. When I came home, nothing was packed and Richard said he had made the phone calls. He gave me the names of people he spoke to and the dates and times of various meeting-places, but said he did not want to go. I did not want to tell Richard what to do or control his life, but I could not live in this insanity. I told him that if he thought he could do it on his own, that would be fine, but this recent event was the final straw; his health matters would no longer preclude me from kicking him out. He said he understood. I never made the mistake of leaving morphine lying around again. Richard never shot his morphine again.

Finding Sanity
A week later, Richard said he was not pleased that I was "controlling his life" regarding the morphine and syringes that were kept in my possession, though he was not angry. Richard never really got angry and he almost seemed afraid of anger. When I got angry, he always quietly said, "I sense some hostility here." I said in this particular circumstance, "I am not trying to control your life; I am taking control of one part of your life that you have no control over. If you want to shoot your morphine you are free to do so – just not here." I told Richard that if he really felt an urge to shoot his morphine, he should tell me so that we could pray about it.

About one week later Richard mentioned that he really wanted to shoot his morphine instead of taking it orally, and I became angry. He said, "I thought you wanted me to tell you when I felt this way?" He was right. I was thankful he felt comfortable enough with me and trusted me to talk about these matters. I apologized. Together, we prayed that his needle addiction would go away. Richard mentioned his desire for needle drugs one more time, but never again after that. About a month went by and I asked him about his addiction, since it had been almost a life-long habit. He told me that it was pretty difficult at first, but that if it came to his faith or the needle, he chose the love of Christ, and that it no longer bothered him. I looked upon his abstinence from needle-addiction as a miracle of healing. I told my son about it, and he said, "At least he will die a free man and have that monkey off of his back." How true. Had Richard not come to live with me, he probably would have been dead shortly after he was released from the hospital, either from an overdose, blood sugar problems, or basically not taking care of himself. He would have died alone as just another statistic, a drug user, in a cheap motel. How sad. Thank you God that Richard meant so much to you.

Richard's sugar bottomed out several times while he was with me, prior to when I took control of his insulin. He took 10-12 units of insulin with each meal and 25 units at bedtime, according to prescribed directions, regardless of how much or what he ate. Several times he took his 25 units at bedtime, without much to eat, and he was almost dead by morning. Twice, I came home at lunch to find his sugar dangerously low. He sometimes forgot if he even took insulin, and occasionally he may have taken a dose twice by accident. We kept pancake syrup and orange juice in the house for these times, when I would literally hold him down while I poured syrup down his throat.

There were a few occasions when his sugar was extremely low and I thought he might choke, or I could not get anything down his throat, so I had to call the paramedics who came with a glucose IV to pump some sugar into him. After he came around and ate something, the paramedics would leave. On one of these occasions, something funny occurred. Richard started coming around and I got him a cup of yogurt to eat so the paramedics could leave. When I brought him the yogurt, he bowed his head and prayed, as we always did before we ate. The paramedics looked at each other and at me, and they asked in wonderment, "What is wrong with him? He was coming around... what is happening?" I laughed and responded that he was praying a prayer of thanks before eating. At that point in time, I knew Richard's heart. After the paramedics left, he said to me, "Good job. Thanks." Richard was grateful to have someone who cared for him. Fortunately, he never had to go to the hospital with one of his diabetic episodes as he had numerous times when he lived alone and someone fortunately found him. When I reminded Richard of the people at the motel who went through his pockets while he was half-conscious and near death in such situations, Richard began to understand my hatred for drug addiction. He was grateful to be in my care, and he told me so often. The doctor told me he had about six weeks to live. Well, I am happy to say that Richard never went back into the hospital, and that I worked on this book you are reading as I sat next to him 12 weeks later. It is amazing what love and the will to live can do to the human spirit.

Hopes Materialized

One of the social workers at the hospital, whom I came to love dearly and who has since been loving and supportive, told me that when I decided to take Richard home, that he would never quit his needle addiction. "I have worked with substance abuse patients and you know there is an 80% relapse rate. He won't quit, you know." Well... he did quit. God may not have healed him from his cancer as we prayed, but He healed him of his addiction. I later reflected on how God did perform miracles. Richard's pain had been managed well, and he never had the pain that some people endure. He took about one-third of the morphine prescribed to him, and he did just fine. He always had a great appetite and he gained about twenty-five pounds since leaving the hospital. He never had nausea or trouble breathing and he was not on oxygen. He did not have liver problems due to his hepatitis. He did not die of his sepsis back in early December. All of the doctors and nurses had been amazed.

A Thirst for Life

Since Richard was released from the hospital, we did those things he said he wanted to do. He even bought a car, and if that made him happy, I was happy. He also bought a tool kit and worked on the car for a while until it got a little too difficult for him physically, and then he hired an unemployed mechanic from the motel where he formerly lived to work on his car to get it running. Richard felt bad that I had to drive him wherever he needed to go, and he was anxious to drive. He said he just wanted to feel normal again and "like a man." He did not want to drive my van, since he preferred driving small cars. I mostly feared for his safety because he was growing weaker and his eyesight was not good, which made driving unsafe.

Since Richard left the hospital, he began to get stronger, gained weight, started walking well, and felt better overall, especially after he stopped the IV drugs. We occasionally visited Chuck and Julie at the motel, and everyone who knew Richard commented on how good he looked and said that I must have been taking good care of him. Richard even talked about getting a part time job to supplement his disability pay, and we talked about trips he wanted to take. Now that he was walking better, he said that maybe he would try to jog with me since I ran each morning. Wouldn't that be something! We thought that maybe, through all of our praying each day, God might give him some health and strength for a while and maybe Richard could live what he called "a normal life" for a while.

One evening, I came home from work and to my surprise, Richard was not home. He was considerate and called me shortly after he knew I would be home. He said he was with Chuck and would be home soon. A couple of hours later I saw a beautiful teal and black convertible Camaro pull up to the apartment. Richard bought another car! I thought he was crazy for doing so, but of course I never told him so. It made him happy, and he was hoping for an extension of life, which we prayed for each morning. I was happy for him. He was excited to show me his new car and we went for a ride the next day when it was bright and sunny. He asked if I liked it, and I told him that I did. "Good," he said, "because I bought it for you. I was hoping you would like it." It was an old car that cost him $3,000. While with his diagnosis I thought this was a silly thing to do, $3,000. was not the end of the world, and it made him happy. It was worth every penny.

Richard was happy. We had taken several rides in the car, and I usually drove. One Saturday, it was warm and sunny, so we took a long drive on a beautiful road out in the country, and we stopped along the way to take some pictures of him in the car. He was so happy and proud of his car. We had fun driving around on nice days with the top down. We both used to ride motorcycles, and during my time with Richard, I did not have one; besides, Richard was too weak to ride a motorcycle, though we would sometimes go to the Harley shop and look around. He still talked about getting one and us riding together. I let him dream… I told him that driving in a convertible was as close as we were going to get to a motorcycle, and he laughed and agreed. We enjoyed our rides together in his new car.

We also went out to eat at Red Lobster, which was one of those little things he had wanted to do with the time he had left. We went to several other restaurants as well, which he really enjoyed. On account of Richards' seemingly new-found health, we also made it to the art museum to see a Monet to Dali exhibit. For years Richard had worked as an artist and we both enjoyed the arts: paintings, poetry, plays, literature, music, etc. We both had a wonderful time touring this art exhibit.

Despite our vastly different lives, we had a lot in common. Richard was still walking when we went to the art exhibit, but he soon grew tired, so we got a wheel chair and he reluctantly used it for the museum tour. We toured the exhibit, and when he got tired a couple of hours later, we left and went next door to Union Station, which he wanted to take me to for a drink. It was a beautiful building. We looked around Union Station, and then we went to a quaint lounge for a glass of Merlot for me and a Wild Turkey & Diet Coke for him. At one time, Richard had a drinking problem and several DUI's, but over the years he conquered his alcohol abuse.

One Friday evening when we were at home, we finished all we had to do and sat down in the living room, each with our bourbon and Coke. He looked at me on this peaceful night and said, "This is nice." It was the simple pleasure of two friends, at peace, enjoying the simple things in life that Richard found so "nice." On account of Richard's cancer, the thought of a bourbon and Coke within a few months came to nauseate him, so his nightly drink came to a sudden halt. So did our hopes.

When Richard was still in the hospital, I used to tell him that I was happy to do even the simplest things with him, such as a walk in our favorite park. With the dog on a leash and him in the wheelchair, we did indeed walk through that park several times. We also went to another park we loved, which is a huge forest preserve area, and we walked there with his wheelchair and the dog on several occasions. Unfortunately, due to his increasingly taxing illnesses, Richard began to lose the desire to go anywhere, and he complained about it being too much trouble for me. I often encouraged him to go places with me, especially on the weekends. Once he understood that it was a joy, and not a burden to spend time out together, he thanked me and said he had a good time and was glad I got him out. I told him I wanted to spend all of my time with him and wanted to see him do as much as he could. He agreed, and was grateful.

One particular Saturday after I encouraged him to go to the park with me and the dog, he said that he wanted to do something for me, since I was always doing something for him; he was so appreciative. "I want to take you to lunch. Do you want me to do that?" I told him that if he was tired not to worry about it, and that maybe we could do something some other time. "I can fix you some lunch at home. Do you want me to fix you something?" "When you are up to it, Richard, I would love for you to fix me some lunch." I told him that I loved his omelets, which were truly about the best I had ever tasted. Richard was a good cook and used to cook on occasion. He made the best cooked carrots I had ever eaten. According to some, he made a delicious meat loaf. It looked good, but being a vegetarian, I did not eat it. Richard made quite a few dishes that were delicious, but when he got weaker, he no longer cooked, and I missed it.

Friends
I met some people at the hospital who quickly became my friends. They reminded me of Richard and me. Daniel was a Harley rider with long hair and tattoos, and Sue was a Christian woman who brought Daniel, her fourth husband, to the Lord. She was widowed three times, and her previous husband died from cancer. We bonded immediately, and they invited Richard and me out to their home in the mountains about three hours away for a weekend. We both thought it would be a good idea to take a couple of days off and get away. Planning to take off the following Monday and Tuesday, we were going to head out for this mini vacation on Saturday. We were packed and ready to go, and Richard was on the couch and said, "You're going to hate me, but I'm just not up to going." After a moment of silence, I said, "Of course I don't hate you. I understand." I was crushed inside, and was so looking forward to a few days in the mountains. I was angry, frustrated, upset, and felt guilty for feeling this way at the same time. I began unpacking and called my friends, half in tears, to tell them that we would not

be coming. She understood all too well. I called work and left a message that I would be at work Monday morning. Richard's health and comfort were, of course, far more important than my hopes for a short vacation.

Family

My son and his girlfriend came out for a weekend in February since there was a "star party" at the forest preserve. My son is fascinated with astronomy, and there were going to be professional astronomers out in the dark woods one night with telescopes that allowed us even to see the rings of Saturn. A friend of mine from Kentucky was also going to be in the area that same weekend for a Physical Therapy conference, so she came over and we all had dinner together before heading out to the woods. It was a chilly night, but not bad compared to the Chicago February's I was used to. We bundled up, got some lawn chairs and sleeping bags, and off we went. I spent most of my time sitting on the lawn chair with Richard, but I was able to sneak off and see some of the amazing sights through the telescope. Richard, who was not overly thrilled with this star party, asked where the drinks and snacks were. He was pretty funny.

When I lived in Illinois, I always had my family over to my house for Easter dinner. I missed those Easters when I moved to Kentucky, and also when I moved even farther south. I told Richard that I wanted to make Easter dinner in Kentucky for my son and his girlfriend. I also wanted to spend Easter Sunday at my church in Kentucky. We made the trip and had a good time. My son thought Richard looked much worse than when he last saw him and he wondered how long Richard had to live. Richard had steadily become weaker and I told him that he did not have to go to church with us, but he insisted on going because he loved the Lord and because it was Easter. I was happy that Richard went to church with us, since Easter is, of course, the biggest celebration of the Christian year, and I wanted him to see what a wonderful church I had back "home" in Kentucky. Easter was in mid-March that year, and Richard was still able to walk, though he depended on a cane. He nodded off and on through the sermon because of his medications, along with the increasing severity of his illnesses, but otherwise he did OK. Richard said that he really enjoyed the service and that he wished we could find a similar church where we lived; I heartily concurred. After church, we all went home to a nice Easter meal.

That next day Richard noticed some things in the house that needed to be repaired, and even though he was sick and weak, he asked me to take him to the hardware store for the parts needed to repair the screen door and the kitchen sink. Out of the goodness of Richard's heart, he fixed both the screen door and the kitchen sink. I was always amazed at Richard's consideration all throughout his illness.

The Beauty of Foot Washing
Later that evening I went to wash Richard's feet, which I did every night since he left the hospital. Because of his diabetes, the fact that he was prone to infection, and also having been a slow healer from both the diabetes and smoking, I washed the incision where his toe was removed each night and wrapped it with clean gauze, as there was still a slight opening in the flesh. That night, when I pulled up his pant leg to remove his socks in order to wash his feet, to my horror I saw a huge bulge on his ankle the size of a tennis ball! I was terrified, and immediately thought perhaps some tumor had grown on his leg. When I grabbed his sock to pull it down so that I could take a look, the bulge burst and it was just a huge water blister. I wondered how or why it appeared, but I was relieved that it was not any kind of tumor. At this point, I had something else to wash each night, which I did for the next two months. When we got back to the apartment after the long Easter weekend, we went to the hospital to have his leg

looked at, and the doctor had Richard come back each week for the next four weeks. Fortunately, Richard's leg never got infected, as I washed and bandaged his leg and feet every night.

Washing Richard's feet each night for months was a lesson learned. Never in a million years did I think I would daily, literally wash someone's feet as Jesus did His disciples, but there is a humble beauty in that action that I will actually value for the rest of my life. I thank God for the privilege of washing Richard's feet. It was a wonderful experience for the both of us. He told his friend Chuck that I washed his feet each night, and I knew it was a special moment for Richard since he realized that he was fully and absolutely loved. I learned that I loved Richard solely for who he was, and not for anything he did for me.

Richard was physically unable to be sexually active and he no longer had a libido, so we did not have any sexual temptations whatsoever that would be normal under our rather exceptional and unconventional circumstances. I was thankful and Richard's limitation actually helped strengthen our relationship because it denied the possibility of deceptive transgression; people so often, and so foolishly, think they are in love with one another when they merely enjoy each other physically. I told Richard that we had a pure love from Christ that did not include sexual temptation to taint or complicate matters since we were not married anyway. It was because of this lack of sexual tension between us that we were able to live together as unmarried, yet Christian, people of the opposite sex, and I was able to truly care for him out of pure, Christian love and hope. Richard was able to love me in return in the same manner that I loved him.

Mother's Day
Mothers Day came along, and once again, I was on call at the

hospital and could not go to Kentucky to see my son. I was depressed. Richard was teary that morning as well. I told him that it was not good that we were both teary and depressed, and that this was no way to spend the day, any day, and especially a holiday. What made the day worse was that it was cool and rainy and we could not do anything outside. Richard loved to shop, so I told him we could go to the mall for the day, and that he could take me out to lunch for Mothers' Day since there was a restaurant there in the mall, which I really enjoyed. He agreed, and off we went to the mall for the day.

Richard wanted to buy a pair of black walking shoes, which he talked about getting for months. He had not walked any distance for a while, as he just walked around the house with a cane or my help. While we were at the mall, he was in a wheelchair. Also, because he had been retaining water for a long time, his feet were always swollen and he had a hard time getting shoes on, so he just wore slippers. At the mall, he wore moccasin slippers, which were tight and difficult to get on, but if Richard wanted to buy some shoes, I did not want to say that I thought he had no real need of them. He still had hopes of a healing, and he wanted to live so much that I dared not take any of his hope away. We went to the restaurant and it was going to be about a thirty-minute wait until we could get a table, so we went and found his shoes. He was happy.

We then returned to the restaurant and had a delicious meal. Richard wished me a happy Mothers Day. He ordered a huge plate of food, but he only ate a small portion of it since his appetite had greatly diminished, so we took most of his dinner home. He was ready to leave and he wanted a cigarette, which he had gone for a couple of hours without. Richard smoked at least two packs a day, so when he wanted a smoke, he *really* wanted a smoke. At this point, I was more than happy to take him outside for a cigarette and to watch him enjoy something.

It is amazing how we change with time and circumstances... I was happy that we got out for the day, and again, Richard thanked me for "dragging him out" so we did not sit in the house all day, teary and depressed.

It is amazing how we change with time and circumstances....

Chapter Six

Walking Through the Gate

The hospital called. A family was about to remove a patient from life support, and he was expected to die quickly. I got to the hospital and ministered to the family and stayed with them when the life support was removed. It seemed like we were all in that room for hours, though only ten minutes passed until he died. The wife could not bear to step through the door and watch him die. The next day was to be their forty-fifth wedding anniversary. The patient had small cell lung cancer, just like Richard. After the final paperwork, I walked out the hospital door and realized that soon I would have to walk through that gate.

Angels

Life went along without major changes for the next couple of weeks, although Richard got weaker and weaker. I noticed one day he had lost a front tooth; he said it just fell out while he was eating. Ironically, the space eventually came in handy, which I will explain later. The couple who wanted us to come out to their home in the mountains for the weekend a few weeks ago was in the area. The lady of the couple called to tell me that her husband just had his one leg amputated right above the knee due to a terrible infection, and that he wanted us to visit. I told her I would try to get Richard out so we could visit them. It was a Saturday in mid May, and I told Richard that it might be nice for him to go to the hospital as a visitor, rather than as a patient for a change. He agreed to go. I got some nice clothes on him, shaved him, brought a pail to him to brush his teeth (so he did not have to stand at the sink), and off we went. He walked down to the van pretty well, though he had to hold on to me just slightly and also used his cane. While we lived on a first floor apartment, the area was hilly so there were still some steps that Richard could no longer handle, but there was a grassy area next to the steps, which is how he got back and forth to the apartment and parking lot.

Richard was quiet and tired when we visited, so we kept the visit short. The couple was happy that we came to visit them and they were thankful to have met Richard, since they had heard so much about him from me. We encountered a major problem when we got back home. Richard got out of the van with my help, took one step, and said he could not walk. We had no way to get him back into the apartment. He leaned against the van and said that he could not walk. For a moment, I looked at him and asked, "Well what are we going to do? How will we get this wheelchair up this hill or these steps?" Completely dumbfounded, I prayed, "God, help me here, because I don't have a clue what to do right now." I looked up, and there were two large Mexican men walking right towards us. I called out, "Excuse me, can you help me here?" They communicated that they did not speak English, but they came right up to Richard, grabbed his arms from both sides, and walked him into the apartment. I could not believe it. They turned and walked away, back from wherever it was they came. Richard was exhausted, and I said, "Well that worked! Thank you God." There was no way these two men could have known our dilemma, heard us talking, or understood what the problem was; I believe God sent angels to help.

Richard's sudden weakness was attributed to low blood pressure. He wore a blood pressure patch, and took oral blood pressure medication, so I removed the patch. We were home and safe. I got Richard to lie down, took off his new shoes, and thanked God for His watchful care. I did not know if those two "men" who assisted Richard were mere men or indeed angels, but I saw how God cares for us. God delights in helping us in strange and unexpected ways.

Deathly Changes
About a week later, I came home and found Richard on the couch with ashes on his forehead. I wondered what had happened and asked, "Richard is that ash on your forehead?" "I don't know," he replied. Richard had been getting confused lately, which was scary for us both. I thought it to be another of those hazy times… yet something told me differently. "Richard, did you fall?" "Yes," he replied, "Where?" "In the hall" he said. Fortunately, there was carpeting and no furniture, so he did not hit his head or hurt himself. He said he had been down for a long time. As always, his cell phone was in his shirt pocket, but he could not figure out how to call me. He said he finally made his way to the couch and barely found the strength to climb onto it. This entire scenario scared me. I felt sorry for him. We both realized that he could not stay home alone anymore. He agreed to my suggestion to have someone stay with him during the day. I was surprised that Richard agreed to hired help since he was a private man and a loner for most of his life. For him to have agreed to this situation, I knew he must be scared. It was time to call Hospice.

Hospice
The Hospice nurse came the next morning. Hospice came to the house to keep Richard from ever going back into the hospital. I made sure each morning that Richard had everything he needed before I left for work, and came home at lunch each day to check on him. Since he had fallen the

previous day, I did not want him to get up unless someone was home with him; he was OK with that situation, though I was a bit nervous. I left a note for the nurse that explained how he had fallen the previous day; I asked her to take him to the bathroom, get him a snack, and make sure he did not leave the bed, and that I planned to be home at noon for the rest of the day.

When I came home, Richard had an uneaten cup of yogurt by the bed. Richard always ate a cup of yogurt mid-morning, often supplemented by a banana. He ate breakfast at 6:15 every morning, but he needed something to eat around 10:00 since he was supposed to eat every four hours with his diabetes. Now that I had the Hospice nurse come three times per week, she would also get him something to eat and do these things for him. Richard did not remember if the nurse had been there that morning. His confusion was getting worse. He was always worried that his cancer would spread to his brain, which lung cancer often does. I would ask him what the dog's name was or where I was from... things he should know, and he would get upset because he sometimes did not remember. Because of his confusion, in addition to his fall, and also his propensity to fall asleep while smoking, I had to hire someone right away to stay with him full time.

The Hospice social worker came with a list of agencies, so I decided to take Friday afternoon off to make phone calls. It was quite expensive, as the local agencies all charged around $17.00 per hour. This expense required all of Richard's disability check, but it had to be done. The only other option was to move him to the Hospice center, which would have been free. I asked what he wanted. He vehemently refused the option of moving away, and said he wanted to stay home with me; so we decided to bite the bullet and spend the money. After all, it was his life.

A Reminder of Mortality

The next day (Saturday), I was "on call" and the hospital called. A family was about to remove a patient from life support and he was expected to die quickly. I told Richard I needed to go to work, and he assured me that he was fine. I called one of the chaplains and asked her if she would come in for me if my call was drawn out; she agreed. It was a difficult call when I found out that the patient who was expected to die had small cell lung cancer, just like Richard. I got to the hospital and ministered to the family, prayed with them, spoke with them, and stayed with them when the life support was removed. It seemed like we were all in that room for hours, though only ten minutes passed until he died. The wife did not come in but was in the waiting room. It was to be their forty-fifth wedding anniversary the next day. Tears flowed freely. After I took them to do some final paperwork, I walked them out to their car and left.

After two and a half hours I ran into the apartment to find an empty bed. I panicked. Had Richard fallen? Was he on the floor? To my relief he was in the bathroom and said, "Oh, good timing. Could you help back to bed?" Of course I would, with great relief. The following night, to my surprise, he got up and went to the bathroom by himself, and then he put himself back to bed. He insisted he was OK.

I took Monday off to meet with the agency that was to stay with Richard during the day. I told the lady from the agency that I needed someone to assist Richard if he needed help walking to the bathroom so that he would not fall, to get him his mid-morning snack, to make sure he did not burn the place down by smoking and falling asleep, and just to keep him company. Richard was also having great difficulty getting up from the couch, and it was now a major task. I did not want him to find himself in a position where he could not get up, or for him to fall in his attempt at rising. I gave a two-week deposit to the agency and I felt much better. They said they would have a lady out the next day.

A Necessary Break

This was the first morning Richard did not eat breakfast. He religiously ate two strips of bacon, two eggs over-easy, and a piece of toast or a biscuit each morning. I was concerned. Richard had to sit on a shower chair while he bathed that morning. He was becoming weaker, but he was still OK. He did not want lunch, which was now really worrying me, since he always had such a big appetite. At about 3:00 p.m., I helped him to the patio since it was a beautiful day. We talked for a while, though Richard was a man of few words. He often said he spoke to me more than he did anyone else, since it was his opinion that most people did not have much to say even though they often talk a lot. I took that as a compliment.

We sat outside for hours and talked. Working on my laptop while Richard chain-smoked, I looked at him, and he suddenly seemed to forget how to light a cigarette. He proceeded to smoke the unlit cigarette. Helping him out of the chair to go to bed, he took one step and said he could not walk. I told him to hold onto the wall while I got the wheelchair. This was the first time he needed the wheelchair in the house. He sat in it for a while, smoked a (lit) cigarette, and then I wheeled him into the bedroom. He said he could walk into the bathroom, though I helped him. He was incredibly weak all of a sudden. He went to bed.

Handing Over Care

The new caretaker came the next morning. Having a caretaker made me feel much better about the whole situation, yet I was nervous about having a stranger care for Richard since I was unsure if the care would be sufficient. When I did meet her, I told the caretaker Richard had gotten considerably weaker all of a sudden and that he had not eaten anything except a banana and a cup of yogurt the previous day, which was a sudden turn of events. He also seemed no longer able to walk on his own.

At lunchtime the caretaker was sitting on the patio smoking. She was told repeatedly that she could smoke in the house, but she said it was against company policy. The patio was right outside of the bedroom and the window was open, but Richard's voice had grown extremely weak and I was unsure if she would be able to hear Richard if he called. She also told me that Richard had called her to take him to the bathroom when she was in the apartment a little earlier, but that she had him use the portable urinal. When I got home at 4:00 p.m., she said Richard had not gone to the bathroom all afternoon. I found Richard's pants and mattress wet. I called the company who employed Richard's caretaker and told them of my unhappiness. They apologized, but as for the smoking, they said it was company policy not to smoke in the customer's house, even if the customer said it was OK. I told the company that Richard was at risk of falling and that it would make more sense for the caretaker to smoke in the house, but the company refused. They said they would send another woman out the next day, so I asked for a non-smoker. I also mentioned Richard's wet pants and mattress, which they were not too happy about either.

Unexpected Pain and Trust
I cleaned up the mess and put Richard in his wheelchair. He sat in the wheel chair for a short while and then wanted to get back to bed; with the washed and scrubbed mattress flipped and clean sheets, I told him I would help him to get ready for bed, and he said, "I'll do anything you want me to do." I laughed and asked, "What?" He said, "I love you and I trust you more than I have ever loved and trusted anyone, and I know you know what you're doing; so, I'll do whatever you want me to do." I hugged him, got him ready for bed, and he quickly fell asleep.

After Richard was in a deep sleep, I went to the drug store about five minutes away to buy adult diapers. Richard dreaded even the thought of adult diapers. He used to tell me that he hoped he never had to wear diapers as he did in the hospital, and I would laugh and tell him that I would change them if he did. He exclaimed, "Don't even say that!" I thought of that when I was in the drug store. I went to sleep and woke up around 3:00 a.m., to find his bed soaked. He no longer had control over his bladder. It was time for the adult diapers. I called Hospice to tell them I would need a hospital bed ASAP. I called work and left a message that I would not be in, since a new caretaker was coming to help with Richard. I thought he was going to die that day because of the difficult sudden changes.

I waited for the new caretaker and the hospital bed, and to help the caretaker get Richard into the new bed so that I could dispose of the old one. The new caretaker was a nice woman, but she basically sat and watched television all day. Each time I ran an errand and returned, she was sitting in the living room watching television, and Richard would be alone in the bedroom. On one of my trips back home I found Richard trying to get out of bed and I told the caretaker that she needed to stay in the bedroom to make sure he was safe. I bought another television for the bedroom. Richard enjoyed the science fiction channel; this way, he could be in either place and watch his sci-fi shows.

Anticipatory Grief
Since his death was approaching rapidly, I began a picture-board for Richard's memorial service, because I would not be emotionally able to make the board after he died. Picking up some photos from the drug store, the new caretaker and I worked on his memorial picture board in the living room, away, though in earshot and in sight of Richard. She commented that I was a strong woman, but I was on autopilot and did not

focus on the sadness that seemed to be devouring all that I was doing. It was difficult to explain.

The hospital bed finally came around 3:00 p.m. and it was set up next to mine. The caretaker and I put a sheet underneath Richard and pulled him onto the bed. Richard was so weak and sick looking, and it was so painful to witness. At least with the bars up on the hospital bed, he would be safe, and there was plenty of padding, plastic, and all kinds of precautions to keep the bed dry. We threw out his old, soiled, wet, cigarette-burned mattress, and brought in the new mattress, fresh sheets, and plump pillows. Life was quickly changing. Richard's caretaker left and I lay in my own bed with the bar of the hospital bed down so I could be close to Richard. In his weakness he leaned over and held me. I cried in his arms.

The chaplain from Hospice called and said he heard there had been some major changes and that he wanted to come out to see Richard. Through my tears, he was told he was welcome but that Richard was no longer able to hold a conversation; Richard was only capable of formulating a couple of words here and there. When the chaplain came, he said that he had a really good conversation just last week with Richard, and that Richard actually asked him to come back. The chaplain said that he recently found out that Richard loved motorcycles, and since the chaplain did as well, he thought he had something in common to talk about. I brought the chaplain into the bedroom and he was surprised at Richard's sudden decline. I asked him to pray with Richard and me, and he spoke to Richard for a few minutes. The chaplain and I went into the living room and talked. I was upset, so it was good to talk with a chaplain.

In the middle of the night, I was awakened to the most hurtful and painful sound I had ever heard. Richard, in a quiet, weak voice, cried out, "Help me. Help me." I turned the light on and went over to find him completely soaked in urine. I cried silently, and told Richard not to worry, and reassured him that I would take care of him. I changed everything and went back to bed exhausted and in tears.

Richard's deteriorating body became little more than skin and bones, and all the water in his legs and feet were gone. He looked so skinny and deathly. It was awful. He still reached out for me and hugged and kissed me, though sometimes he would push me away immediately after an embrace. I am not sure what that was all about.

His caretaker became much more conscientious and she attended well to Richard's needs. I asked her if she would sit in the bedroom with him during the day, and she agreed. When I came home for lunch, she was in the bedroom watching television. She said that she had changed him several times, and that all was OK. I still checked his blood pressure and blood sugar and did whatever was needed to keep the sugar level in his body as close to normal as possible. The Hospice nurse had come that same day and told me that Richard's new caretaker was attentive to Richard and took good care of him while she was there. I felt at ease. Since Richard continually wet himself, I arranged to have someone come out five times per week, beginning the next week, to bathe him and to change his bed during the day. I was thankful for all the help.

The Need for Friends
One of the Occupational Therapists approached me at work and asked how I was doing. I did not know her well, but we always said hello at work and had small talk now and then. She had been looking at me with concern and said that I did not appear like myself, but I told her that I was OK. When she approached me that morning and asked what was going on, I began to tear up and told her what was happening. She gave

me her phone number, told me to call her, and she planned to come to my apartment over the weekend so I could get out of the house. I told her I did not need to leave for long, but that I did need to run errands and grocery shop, so if she could sit with Richard for an hour so I could do those things, I would greatly appreciate it. She happily agreed to help. We hugged, and I went home.

When I came home that Friday, I told Richard that I would be with him for the next several days, and he smiled and said, "Good." I spent most of those next days in my bed, and I worked on this book next to Richard. I was frustrated, angry, upset, sad – so many emotions all at once – that it was exhausting. Richard still drank a lot of water and was able to swallow, and he still ate a cup of yogurt every day, but that was all. He was so thin.

Saturday morning I called D., the occupational therapist, and she came right over with a book to read while I ran errands. When D. walked into the bedroom, she introduced herself and sat on my bed, which was next to Richard's. He pulled up the sheet to cover his diaper. She told me to go for as long as I needed, but I did not want to leave Richard for long. I went and did what was needed and came back a couple of hours later. She was sitting on my bed reading and being attentive to Richard. I was happy. It was so nice to have her help. So often, well meaning people ask what they can do, or tell you to call them if you need anything, which for me is difficult to do; but this woman just said she was coming over to help and she allowed me to take care of the things I needed to do. I so greatly appreciated her.

Fading Hopes
I bought Richard some yogurt and ice cream that he always enjoyed. I hoped he would at least eat a cup of yogurt each day to sustain himself. It was so nice to have a friend come

over and give me some relief and some company. This whole thing with Richard was getting incredibly difficult emotionally, especially since I was alone. Surprisingly, Richard said he wanted to get out of bed and into the wheelchair. I got him a pajama top, picked him up, and happily put him in the chair and wheeled him to the kitchen where D. and I were. To my surprise he asked for a cigarette. I gladly lit one for him and gave him a cup of yogurt. As much as I hated Richard smoking, he had not had a cigarette in days, so this craving made me think he might be feeling a little better. He sat in the kitchen with us for about an hour and then he was ready to go to bed. My friend D. left and said she would come back to visit and to help. I thanked her over and over and told her she was welcome in my home anytime. She was most gracious. I spent the remainder of the day just being with Richard.

That night, Richard began to sigh with each exhalation, and his belabored breathing kept me awake. It frustrated me, not knowing what was happening; he seemed so physically and mentally agitated. I was up most of the night as I checked and re-checked everything. I gave him water and morphine. What was happening? He occasionally pulled his knees up to his chest and told me his legs were stiff, so I would rub them. I was doing everything I could to try to comfort him, but it was just not enough. By morning, he was still agitated, and I sat in the bedroom most of the day and worked from my bed, rubbed his legs and I made sure to stay near him. However, by afternoon, I thought that there must be something I could do for him that I might not have done, so I called the Hospice nurse and she soon came to the apartment.

The nurse was not sure what was occurring, since Richard's blood pressure was good, his respiration was normal, his pulse was strong, and his lungs still sounded good. Richard had developed some jelly-like substance that oozed from his eyes, and she thought oxygen might be needed since Richard groaned with each exhalation. The nurse called the pharmacy and had some eye drops and oxygen sent over. I gave Richard water to drink, which he kept reaching for, and the nurse was surprised to see that he was still drinking and swallowing with no problem. I later tried, rather unsuccessfully, to get the eye drops in and to put the oxygen hose in his nose, which he tolerated, though not for long. He kept taking the oxygen off of his face, so I assumed he did not really need it. He slept a little better than the previous night. I fell asleep for a while.

Memorial Day
The next day was Memorial Day, so I was home for the holiday. Richard was extremely agitated again, so I went through all I knew to do, but this particular day he could not drink or swallow, so I used sponges to moisten his mouth, as well as Chapstick. His urine output was down. He still reached out to hug me, and he asked to stand up, which I thought was unusual since he was so weak. However, I stood him up as he requested. He seemed to want to hug me and to feel the warmth of a tight embrace. I held him for about thirty seconds, and then he slowly slumped back to the bed. After I laid him back down, he attempted to give me a kiss. He tried to speak, but His mouth did not move; I knew what he as trying to do, so I kissed him. It was our final kiss. I later realized he had attempted to say goodbye. I continually told him how much I loved him and that whenever he did eventually go to Heaven, I would have a beautiful service for him on earth. I told him that the greatest thing in life was to love and to be loved, and that he surely had that love from God and from me. He nodded in agreement and tried to smile.

His agitation quickly increased. I called Hospice again, and said I did not know what more I could do. That evening, another nurse came and checked Richard's blood pressure, respiration and lungs, and said that everything was still strong. She said he had "terminal agitation" which most people get when they are in the process of dying, so she ordered liquid Ativan and morphine to be administered in a final hope to take away any pain and for him to relax and be at ease. He kept his teeth tightly clenched, so that space where his tooth had fallen out a couple of weeks prior to his final decline came in handy; the medicine was dropped into that space. I thanked God for having that tooth fall out! I began to give Richard a couple of doses of each of the medications, and the nurse left when he finally settled down and fell asleep.

I was hesitant about going to work the next day, but told Richard I would be around if he needed me, that a woman would be with him during the day, and that he would receive a visit from his nurse. I also told Richard that if he got a glimpse of Heaven, that he should just go. I said goodnight. I did not want to let him go, nor would I ever have been ready, but I could not stand to watch him in this agitated condition. I was physically and emotionally exhausted from the last three days. I turned the light off and, in my exhaustion I was ready to go to sleep. Suddenly, I heard a loud rattle from his throat – the death rattle. I prayed that God would take him this night. I was not ready to let him go; I was *never* ready to let him go... but I knew with these sudden, awful changes in the last few days, that he was indeed close to death. I could not stand to watch him suffer, nor did I want him to die while I was at work. I wanted to be with him, close to him... I wanted to hold him... but I was so upset, scared, numb, partially in denial, unable to deal with what was happening, and in my exhaustion, I turned and fell asleep.

A Good Death
Around midnight, I woke up and it was quiet. I turned on the light to find Richard – gone. He simply faded away, like he said he would. I always thought when this moment came I would panic and go crazy, but I felt such a peace as I walked through that gate, and in my spirit I heard God say, "You did

what I sent you here to do," which was to take care of Richard, love him, and not let him die alone. Despite the fact that he had passed away, Richard looked so much better than he had during his last days on the earth. He looked peacefully asleep. He looked like a beautiful angel. Most of the dead bodies at the hospital look ugly and dead, but Richard did not look dead at all. His eyes were tightly shut, and he appeared peaceful. He was like a graceful giraffe in the background of my dream, with the evilness and ugliness of death in front of me. I gave him hugs and kisses, and then I began to cry quietly. I sat and looked at him for a while, and then I called Hospice to tell them that he was gone. They said they were sorry. I knew they were supposed to take care of the details, but I did not know what was going to happen. I sat in the bedroom and just looked at him for about thirty minutes. I then heard a car door slam. It was that last nurse who was at our home. I opened the door, and she hugged me as I sobbed. The nurse said she did not expect Richard to die this night. She knew it would be soon, but had no idea it would be *this* soon. She said that she came to pronounce his death and to make the phone calls for me so that I did not have to do so. I gave her the phone number of the crematory that was going to cremate Richard's body, and we sat in the kitchen and talked for a while as we waited.

The Finality of Death
Around 2:30 a.m., a white van showed up to get Richard's body. We went over some paperwork, I signed a few papers, and the undertaker went into the bedroom. I asked him to leave so I could have a minute alone. I hugged and kissed Richard. The undertaker then covered his body with a sheet and a blanket. I left the room and the undertaker and the nurse put his body onto the stretcher and took it away. I cried hard because I knew it was the last time on earth I would see Richard. It finally hit me. When the nurse left, I cried myself into exhaustion until I fell asleep.

I called work and left a message as to what happened and to inform my boss that I would be off for the week as I prepared to go to Kentucky to do a Memorial service for Richard at my church. Around 6:30 a.m., the head staff chaplain called to tell me he got my message; he expressed his sympathy and told me to take whatever time I needed. The chaplain then informed me that he would see me when I came back. I was a little surprised, since the chaplains at the hospital where I worked did not appear to be very supportive of how I had cared for Richard by taking him to my home to live and to die. I got up and called my pastor in Kentucky, and he suggested Thursday evening for a service at the church. I agreed, and then I called my son and a few friends. Life was forever changed.

I went to the hospital to leave some notes with the chaplains to visit my regular patients and to let them know that I would not be in all week. I then went to the Decadent Affairs office to see V. to pick up Richard's American flag. This trip was difficult for me since it is the office I often took family members to when a patient died in order for the surviving family to sign the various release forms for the possession of the body and to instruct them regarding the accompanying procedures. V. was kind and gave me the flag that I would drape over a table for Richard's memorial service. V. gave me a hug and talked to me as a friend, rather than the chaplain, which I appreciated. I then dropped off Richard's beautiful new wheelchair at the Hospice center since the hospital said they could not take it back. I thought about saving it in case someone from the family needed it, but I did not want it around and Hospice had been so good to me that I wanted to give something nice to them.

Next, I went to the embalming office to pick out an urn for Richard's ashes. They normally put the ashes in a biodegradable plastic urn for burial or immediate spreading, but since Richard wanted his ashes scattered with mine, I needed to get something more permanent until that time. Richard had once asked me if I would spread his ashes with mine, but I told him I did not think I would be the one doing that, and that I would let my son know! We had both laughed.

When I walked into the room with the urns, my eyes immediately went to one particular urn. It was a golden color, and Richard liked only gold jewelry (not silver), with black stripes that had an almost Egyptian look to it. Richard and I were both fascinated with Egyptian culture and we had both thought about being archeologists at one point in our childhood so that we could study ancient Egypt. Also, Richard told me about a strange dream he had while in the hospital: he was kidnapped by some nurses and they dressed him up like an Egyptian person, along with eye make up and a gold medallion that was placed on his forehead. It was a very strange dream. I thought I would honor Richard by buying the Egyptian-looking urn. It seemed strange to me that I thought of all of these things as I picked out an urn. I left and headed for my home in Kentucky.

Back Home in Kentucky
My son was home and his girlfriend had come over that day as well, since they were waiting for me; they both came and gave me big hugs. It was nice to be with family and to feel love. My son had dinner waiting for me on the stove, which was very good. I ate, and my son's girlfriend poured me a glass of wine. I was home, though the last several times I was there I brought Richard with me and I almost expected him to be there somehow. That night, after I went to bed, I had a very restless and disturbed sleep. I was pretty tired and I fell asleep rather quickly, though I did not sleep well. I kept waking up to the echoing memory of Richard's voice that called for help or asked for water. I kept reaching over to

turn the lamp on that was next to my bed in my apartment in State X, though there was no lamp next to me in Kentucky. I continued to turn over to see Richard, and I wondered where he was. I could not figure out where I was and why I could not see Richard. It finally occurred to me, as I began to wake up, that I was alone in Kentucky, and that Richard was not there; this straining scenario continued throughout the night.

I spent the next day cleaning the house and doing yard work. We worked on the yard and got caught up with things that needed to be done, and it was good to take my mind off of my shroud of sadness.

My pastor called me to talk about the service we were going to have for Richard, and I filled him in on some things I wanted to do (such as the presentation of the eulogy, etc.). We were all set for Thursday evening at 6:00 p.m. I was so surprised when the worship leader of the church called me to inform me that he was going to play the music for the service since I had not asked him to do that, and I did not even know the worship leader all that well. I was thrilled that my pastor had asked this musician to do the music and that he had agreed. The worship leader asked if I had any requests, and I told him that I brought a CD since I had not anticipated him doing this wonderfully kind act for me. I wanted a song played from the CD, and I wanted him to play another song on his guitar and to sing "When it's All Been Said and Done" by James Cowen. I chose that particular song not only for its beauty, but for one particular line that says, "Lord, Your mercy is so great, that You look beyond our weakness, and find purest gold in miry clay, making sinners into saints." It then goes on to say, "And I will always sing Your praise, here on earth and ever after; for You've shown us Heavens' our true home, when it's all been said and done – You're our life when life is gone." He told me that he did not know the song but that he would learn it that very night. I told him that I did not want him to work so hard, and to just play something that he already knew, but he insisted that he would meet my request. I was amazed at his kindness. He then said that the pastor suggested we all sing something together, and he asked what I would like to have us sing. I suggested, "It is Well with My Soul," which I have always loved; he said he knew that song well.

The Memorial Service
The next day, we took care of a few more things and got ready for the Memorial service. My son and his girlfriend and I loaded up my van and went to church. I had some friends come to the church, as well as my friends Terry and Margie who owned and ran the animal sanctuary that I had formerly worked at, which was about a 45-minute drive away from the church; their kindness really touched me. Margie, the owner of the sanctuary, brought me some beautiful wild flowers that she had picked from their farm in a glass vase; she was so kind, and Richard would have loved them. My son's girlfriend brought a tripod for me to set pictures on and we draped the American flag over a table. On two other tables, I placed Richard's Vietnam Veterans hat, a cross, some pictures, and other items that were significant to Richard. The pastor and his wife brought some flowers arranged in a stately glass vase which were gorgeous and which greatly surprised me.

The associate pastor also came; he was to fold the flag with my son at the end of the service while TAPS played in the background. We took our seats, and the service began. The first song was played from the CD I brought, and the pastor opened with prayer. The worship leader had us stand and sing together; he then played my song request so wonderfully that it seemed as if he had been playing it for years. I was amazed. Pastor Steve spoke on Luke 15 about the lost sheep, which, of course, was a theme that defined the majority of Richard's life. I had asked Steve if he would speak on Luke 15, and he did a wonderful job. Thank God Richard was found, and heaven rejoiced! Thank God that Richard died a clean, sober, and free man! Pastor Steve spoke about Richard like he had known him his whole life and he said that he loved Richard since I loved him. Pastor Steve honored Richard with deep dignity and respect. I was proud of Richard, my pastor, and this wonderful church. When it was time to do the eulogy, I became worried that I would cry through the whole thing, but I did not. I made it all the way through until the last few lines. Here is my eulogy.

The Eulogy

Richard was born 60 years ago in East Tennessee. His mom and sister both died of cancer while he was a young man and his dad died of a sudden heart attack while he was young as well. Richard died of lung cancer very late at night on Memorial Day, which was quite fitting for a Veteran. He never had any children and was pretty isolated, which surprised me since he seemed to enjoy people and since he was incredibly friendly. He worked as an artist for a while and he loved the Arts (paintings, poetry, and literature); he quoted Shakespeare, Poe, and the Bible. He loved plays, music, movies, and science fiction. He was a very good cook who also enjoyed eating out, though his favorite food seemed to be KFC. He loved to shop (which I hate), and he loved motorcycles. He wanted us to get some motorcycles since I used to ride as well, but he was not strong enough for us to do that. He loved his new car that he just bought three months ago, hoping to live and drive it (a 1994 Camaro convertible). Richard wanted to live.

He was incredibly kind, gentle, tender, polite, forgiving, meek, humble, and peaceful, which is why I wrote, on my picture memorial board, the verse from scripture, "Blessed are the peacemakers, for they shall see God." Richard is seeing God right now. Even when he was sick, not feeling well, or in pain, he never complained, and he remained very considerate, kind, and polite; he always said "please" and "thank you." He was a quiet man of few words, who was always thinking of others. When he came to my house here in Kentucky just a couple of months ago, weak and sick, he wanted to fix a few things around the house, such as a broken screen door and a leaky kitchen faucet, which he did. He asked me to take him to the hardware store so he could buy the parts we needed. He made some food for us. He helped my son bury my one dog, who had just died, behind our garage so I would not have to do it since he knew I loved that dog. He did not think about himself very often, and he was never crabby or short-tempered all through his illness. He always wanted to do things for me, though his weakness prevented him, but he did as much as he could and he always expressed his desire to do things for me. Richard taught me how to live, and how to die.

He was a Vietnam veteran who struggled most of his life with depression and addictions. He went to prison shortly after his return from Vietnam and served 14 years and 7 months of a 25 year sentence. He was released early for good behavior. He accepted Christ as his Savior while in prison through a prison chaplain. He had nothing to do in prison, so he picked up a Bible that was in his cell and began reading it, but said he did not fully understand it. The chaplain helped him, and he and some fellow Christian inmates would read together and act out the stories in the Bible as if they were putting on a play. He was baptized at a Church of

Christ while he was in prison. Richard said the first person he wants to meet when he gets to Heaven is the disciple John. I asked him why, and he replied that the Bible says that is the disciple Jesus loved, and he wants to know what it was about John that made Jesus love him so.

Richard bounced around in life and was homeless for a few months at one point, when he could not work and his disability did not come in a timely manner. When I asked him what it was like to be homeless, he said, "It wasn't that bad." Like I said, he never complained or felt sorry for himself. Before coming to live with me, he lived alone in a cheap motel room where one pays week to week; he was diagnosed with cancer within this past year, around October. He stayed in the hospital from October until January, after doing one round of chemotherapy that almost killed him, and he developed an infection in his heart and blood and a gangrene big toe that was amputated in November. I can't believe he lived for as long as he did since his last hospitalization, for he was incredibly sick. God is good and He gave him another chance.

While he was in the hospital those three months, his rent was not paid, so all of his earthly possessions were tossed outside for anyone to take, and then thrown away. The other people who lived at the motel knew these things were Richard's, but being drug addicts, they pawned, kept, or sold his things. When he finally got out of the hospital in early January, I got him a coat so he could go outside without freezing, and we went to the motel to see if there was anything left. When he discovered everything he had was gone, he did not get angry, but just looked at me and said, "Well I guess we need to go shopping." We shopped at the thrift stores and Goodwill/Salvation Army, and he was happy.

One night, after dinner, he asked me about Heaven and if I thought there would be animals there. "Of course," I replied. "God made the animals before He even made us, and they were there in the Garden, so I think they will be in Heaven. Why do you ask?" Richard said that before he got out of prison, he served the last part of his sentence as a worker at a state ranch and he had a horse there he called Spunky. He would go down to the creek when his work was done, with the horse and talk to him; he really loved that horse. He wanted to see Spunky again. I suddenly had a thought; "Richard," I said, "I believe you will see that horse again when you get to Heaven, and I believe that when I get there you will meet me on that horse, pull me up behind you on the back of that horse, and we will ride together." He had tears streaming down his face, and so did I.

Richard was assured of his salvation, but he said he wanted to live longer, as he "kind of liked it here" on earth and wanted to be with me. I told him I wanted him to live longer as well, as I loved him very much and wanted to live with him too. He told me and my son that if he was not "living this nightmare" (referring to his cancer) that he would ask me to marry him. I would have gladly married Richard. He said he was finally living a "normal" life, and he wished he had met me 40 years ago. Only problem with that, I told him, is that he would have been twenty years old and I would have been six! Not too normal. He laughed, and said, "Well maybe more like twenty five years ago!" We wanted a life together and actually talked about plans and dreams we made if he somehow could live. We wanted to get a log cabin on some land with a small river or creek on it in order to swim and to just enjoy life with each other.

One of my former seminary professors said to me recently when I told her about Richard, "There is truly nothing more miraculous and powerful than to love and be loved in utter weakness. God's love came to us not in strength and power, but in humility and sacrifice." That is how Richard loved. Richard inspired me to write this book. My dedication for the book is to Richard, "Who gave me the courage to love... even when you have no idea what is waiting around the corner. Thank you, Richard. I will always love you with a love that even the angels covet." My life is richer for having known and loved you, Richard. Thank you. And Richard... pick me up on your horse when I get home; I'll see you then... and take me to Jesus.

Lessons in Death
I cried a bit on that last paragraph. My church made me a CD of Richard's memorial service, so, at some point, I could listen to it again when the deep pain begins to fade. Richard was one of "the least of these" that the Bible talks about (according to society), but he was someone I learned far more from than any seminary professor or pastor. He taught me how to love with a pure heart, and like the "sinners" in the Bible, he showed how thankful he was and how much he loved because as Scripture says, "...the one to whom little is forgiven, loves little," (Luke 7:47), and therefore to whom much is forgiven, loves much. Richard, when given the ultimatum of love or his drug addiction, chose the grace, mercy, and love of Jesus, and the love of a friend. He chose the one thing he

wanted all along in life – love. I asked him that if he could live his life over again and do whatever he wanted to do, what or who would he choose to be. He told me that he would have liked to have been a pastor; his response did not surprise me, and he would have made a good one. I wonder if that was what God had in mind for him.

I ran across a woman at the hospital whose husband had been there for a long time with cancer. She got to know Richard, and had heard through a neighbor who was also in the hospital with Richard that he came to live with me until the end. She heard Richard had passed away, and she said that she was so grateful he was not alone when he died. She said that Richard had told her, at one point, that he knew he did not have long to live and that he was all alone. She said Richard seemed pretty depressed about it all. He told her that at least he would not leave behind a wife and kids who would miss him. That was the way Richard thought – always of others. Little did he know at that time that he would leave me behind... someone who loved him and who misses him tremendously.

The week after I returned from Kentucky following his memorial service, some of the nurses who cared for Richard asked me how he was doing. Through tear-filled eyes, I told them that he died. They all commented on how much they liked him, how kind he was, and how he never complained. When my son recalled my teaching concerning the fact that nature revives each year in a manner similar to the resurrection, he wrote this statement about Richard: "He was like a flower whose once supple petals unfortunately became a hardened shell... a man whose sweet scent became choked by the smog of disillusionment. Yet, Richard was a man who was loved by the Almighty, and through the Almighty's death and resurrection, Richard's hardened shell was transformed back into the supple petals that were originally intended. He was a man whose sweet scent eventually overcame the smog of others' disillusionment. Richard was a man who loved the Almighty. Near the conclusion of his life, Richard was revived by the Almighty, and in His death, by His resurrection, I am confident that Richard will be raised by the Almighty to inherit everlasting life." **Richard was a beautiful man!**

**Richard taught me how to live,
and how to die.**

Chapter Seven

Learning About Turning Stones

When I read about "turning stones," it was not clear what the author meant. Near the end of Marc Parent's book, he wrote about a nun traveling in remote places who turned over stones as she went. Someone asked why she turned over stones, and her response opened my eyes. She explained that turning over a stone was a tangible way to say something is different because she was there. I think about her response often. Should not places and people be different because we were there? It is never too late to turn over a stone in someone's life, even in their dying days.

Turning Stones
I read a book several years ago written by Marc Parent called, *Turning Stones*. It is a story about his work as a caseworker in the city of New York, and the nightmare of the lives of so many people. His job was to physically remove children from their homes when they were in harmful situations. Throughout the book, I could not understand why he titled the book as he did, since I did not understand anything about "turning stones" and how that fit into his work. Near the end of the book, there was an abrupt chapter about some nuns who were traveling

and he mentioned one particular nun who always walked into some remote place on their tours and turned over a stone. When someone finally asked why she did that, she said it was a physical, tangible way to say that something was different because she had been there and a reminder that life should indeed be different because she was there. That chapter has been imprinted on my mind and I think about it often. Is that not how we should live our lives? Should not our lives, and therefore our deaths, have an impact on others? Should not places and people be different because we were there? I pray, in a small way, that my short time with Richard impacted his life. Richard's life, which, according to him was "wasted" for many years in addictions and crime, certainly had an impact on me. It is never too late to make an impact or to turn a stone on this earth, even in one's dying months. Richard's attitude, consideration, and kindness, in the midst of pain and suffering, turned stones for me and forever changed my perspective on living and dying.

God's Grace

Richard used to tell me that all of his family died young; he was the only one who abused himself with drugs and alcohol, yet he lived longer than any of them. I told Richard that I looked at the length of his life as God's perfect organization and grace, since Richard needed to experience real love before he died, and, *more importantly*, he needed to experience God's unbelievable grace and forgiveness. God was patient with Richard and He gave him time to get his affairs in order before he died. God also allowed Richard to feel complete trust and love for and from another human being before he died, which is a wonderful gift. I think of the verse in 2 Peter 3:14-15, which says, "Therefore, beloved, since you look for these things, be diligent to be found by Him in peace, spotless and blameless, *and regard the patience of our Lord to be salvation*" (italics mine). I believe the Lord had unbelievable patience with Richard and that He knew his heart, which of course God knows all of our hearts, and that He allowed Richard more time to run into me, who showed him true, genuine agape love and who helped point the way back to his Savior. God is truly patient and loving, and His mercy certainly does endure forever. Isaiah 30:18 says, "Therefore the Lord waits to be gracious to you; therefore he will rise up to show mercy to you;" God surely did that for Richard. God sent His Son Jesus to seek and save the lost, but Richard had indeed lost his way since his conversion way back in the 1970's while in prison. Richard was that lost sheep. God, in His unfathomable mercy, gave Richard another chance and allowed him to live long enough to come back home. What a loving God we serve!

God's Healing
I wanted to see Richard healed or at least be given more time for several reasons. I wanted Richard to be healed for his own sake because he wanted to live, to love, to make up for so many wasted years, to do some good, and to "live a normal life." As our relationship changed while we were together, we went from friends, to good friends who loved one another, to two people who loved deeply and wanted to be husband and wife. We wanted to get married, go to Kenya and meet my friends who had been praying for him. We wanted to do ministry together, and live a wonderful, Christian life as man and wife. I wanted him to have that chance, but at his death, I realized that we are given each day as a gift from God. Since we do not know the length of our days here on earth, we need to make the most of each one.

I loved Richard and wanted a lot more time with him. I wanted those fifteen years we prayed for each day, like those extra years God gave Hezekiah. I know God can heal. I know He has and does heal, both in the Bible, and in our world today. I also know that sometimes He chooses *not* to heal, as with the apostle Paul who prayed for his "thorn in the flesh" to go away, but God did not heal him from that affliction (II Corinthians 12:7-9). I think about Hebrews 9:27 that says, "And inasmuch as it is appointed for men to die once and after that comes judgment..."; this passage tells me that we only have one life on earth – that's it – and we need to make the best of it and live up to the potential God so mercifully gave us. When Richard prayed for salvation and was baptized in prison, I wondered why he did not follow the Lord when he got out... why he fell away and stayed away from the Lord until we ran into one another at the hospital.

Asking God to bring revival to the area and specifically to the hospital was my frequent prayer. Can you imagine what would have taken place spiritually had Richard been healed, a man no one really cared about and who the medical staff was just basically waiting for his death? Can you imagine what Richard would have felt and possibly have become? Why don't these things happen? I know they do in other parts of the world, and Richard and I believed that God could heal him if He so chose. God merely chose not to, and God is always right. However, Richard did experience other healings which were mentioned earlier in this book. Any time we were at a church and they had a healing service, Richard and I were there. When the pastor called people to be anointed with oil for a physical healing, Richard got there as quickly as he could. Richard believed in healing, and he so wanted to be healed. He wanted to live. I often anointed Richard with oil, both at the hospital chapel and at home, as we prayed for a healing. We prayed daily for those fifteen years of life, even while we watched him grow weaker. Richard was healed of his addictions and he was set free, and I do believe he was healed on past occasions, and that he was granted more life. We needed to accept God's will when he was not healed of his cancer; we all die, and apparently this was Richard's time.

Free Will

Why is there death in this world? Why so much pain and suffering, sickness and grief? Those who are Christian believe that it is because of the fall in the Garden of Eden. Sin, death, and all of the grief, sadness, and pain that accompanies sin came as a result of disobedience, pride, and lack of belief in what God said. The whole problem of theodicy, believing in a good God with all the evil in the world, is nothing but the result of God having given us free will. I have a dear friend who said when she gets to Heaven the first thing she wants to ask God is why He gave us free will in the first place? All we did with it was eat too much, drink too much, abuse ourselves, hurt others, and die. Sometimes I feel the same way, but then I try to bring it into human terms that I can understand, and I am thankful for our free will. I am thankful Richard *chose* to live with me while he was sick, for I never forced him to stay. I am thankful Richard *chose* to give up his needle addiction for the sake of the faith, for he knew he had formerly been a slave to his addictions rather than a slave to Jesus Christ. Through our multifaceted relationship, Richard was able to choose God's redemptive love over his own self-destructive habit. Isn't that what we do when we completely turn our lives over to God, when we say, "Not my will Lord, but Yours," as Jesus taught us to say? And what did Richard get in return for his choice of love? - Someone to love him deeply and care for him greatly until his final breath. What did he leave behind with that choice? - dying alone as a junkie and as another statistic, suffering miserably by himself, or if he was fortunate, being found suffering alone in his room, and being taken by ambulance to die alone in a hospital room with no one to give him a memorial service or even care that he was gone. Yes God, we mess up daily, but thank You for free will!

Evil

With free will came the opportunity for evil, which, as we all know, came with a vengeance. While death is a normal part of life, it was not originally meant to be and so death is still our enemy which Jesus will conquer. Unfortunately, "The wages of sin is death" (Romans 6:23). Death is a result of evil. Many well-meaning people say some hurtful things after a death because they do not really know what to say. Please, say nothing. I have heard people talk about the "redemption" and "peace" of death after an illness. For those of us left behind who feel great loss and grief, there is no redemption – just pain. Illness and death are ugly. I watched a handsome man turn into a man that I barely knew (physically). The evil of sickness and death had taken over Richard's body and face. When I looked upon him and his deteriorating body, I began not to get angry at God, but to love God all the more, as I knew these changes were something God hated as well, for He came to earth to conquer and destroy death. I began to understand what it means to "hate evil" (Amos 5:15), as I could clearly see what evil does to us – it destroys and kills us. Evil manifests itself, I believe, as we die. Though we cannot change what evil does to us physically, we can decide what it will do to us spiritually, mentally, and emotionally. While Richard did not embrace his sickness and dying, he did handle it with courage, consideration, love, and gratefulness... which is where I believe that redemption manifests itself in opposition to evil. Richard may have made a lot of mistakes throughout his life, but in the last moments, he got it right.

My father once told me as he walked through a nursing home, and looked at the weak, sick, and dying people in that place, he thought, "Thank God there *is* death." Can you imagine living in such a state forever? I am grateful Richard did not suffer physically for long. While I watched Richard die, I too thought, "Thank God for death"; but more so... much more so... I say, "Thank God for eternal life, where we will all be together, healthy and whole, with no more sickness and death, as we will be 'more than conquerors through him who loved us'" (Romans 8:37).

Pain and Joy

Richard's diagnosis was know by me from the beginning of our journey, and I am most grateful God sent me to the south to care for him and to keep him from being alone, though I sometimes get upset that we could not have had years together. I had great pain and emotional suffering after his death, as all people do when they lose someone they love. I was not (and am not) angry with God, but I did wish Richard and I could have had more time together.

C. S. Lewis wrote in his classic book, *The Problem of Pain:*

> When I think of pain – of anxiety that grows like fire and loneliness that spreads out like a desert, and the heartbreaking routine of monotonous misery, or again of dull aches that blacken our whole landscape or sudden nauseating pains that knock a man's heart out with one blow, of pains already intolerable, and then are suddenly increased, of infuriating scorpion-stinging pains that startle into maniacal movement a man who seemed half dead with his previous tortures – it 'quite o'ercrows my spirit'
>
> (Lewis,1965).

Yes, I felt those deep crushing pains, and I still feel that "dull ache" that Lewis described, but I also feel the loving presence of a God who loved Richard and me, for He loves all people, and He also hates death, as we do. Through this experience, I see how much God loves us and how much He loves one individual at a time, such as Richard, for He set up the remainder of Richard's life so that he was cared for and loved.

I asked Pastor Steve to read Luke 15:4-7 at Richard's memorial service, which reminded me of Richard and God's great love for him. Jesus said,

What man among you, if he has a hundred sheep and has lost one of them, does not leave the ninety-nine in the open pasture, and go after the one which was lost, until he finds it? And when he has found it, he lays it on his shoulders, rejoicing. And when he comes home, he calls together his friends and his neighbors, saying to them, 'Rejoice with me, for I have found my sheep which was lost!' I tell you that in the same way, there will be more joy in heaven over one sinner who repents, than over ninety-nine righteous persons who need no repentance.

Richard had accepted Christ many years ago in prison, but he wandered away and did not live the life of a Christian until the end. He was one of the lost sheep that Jesus went after.

When Richard prayed with me in that hospital chapel and at my home, there was great rejoicing in Heaven. Richard died in peace and entered Heaven, and I think of Luke 15 regarding the Prodigal Son; there was not only great rejoicing in Heaven, but a banquet given in honor of Richard's homecoming, as there will be for us all. The peaceful look about Richard at his death is a look I will never forget. It was as if, for the first time, he was finally at total peace, with no more demons to fight... no more addictions or depression... no more loneliness or sorrow. The sting of death is gone for those who die in Christ, but I am sure feeling its sting in my grief and loneliness. How on earth do people face death and grieve the loss of a loved one without the hope of eternity and God's saving love? I cannot even begin to image how they cope.

God's Organization

My dear Kenyan friend Nathan Chesang enjoys saying, "God is very organized." God certainly is. I think about the timing of my arrival at the Veterans' hospital for my CPE Residency. I applied to many hospitals, and was met with closed doors. Also, since I had a trip planned to go to Kenya for a couple of weeks in November, I was told I could not begin until the following year, since I would miss too much time. Richard came into the hospital shortly after I returned from Kenya, and he remained there for the next several months, isolated and alone, all while he knew that he was dying. I was also the chaplain given all three of the wards that Richard was on as he moved around in the hospital. It was as if God picked me up from Kentucky and dropped me down farther south so I would be there for him in his final months.

The timing of Richard's death made it possible for us to spend his last days together, since I was home Friday afternoon and all of a three-day holiday weekend. The night he died, his blood pressure, heart rate, and respiration were still strong, and his lungs were clear, but it was as if he knew that I was in a panic about going back to work and leaving him with strangers. I prayed that I would be home with Richard when he died, and he died late that very night in the hospital bed right beside my bed.

At the same time, when life would be painful and going back to work difficult, we had three summer chaplain interns come that previous week, who took three of my four wards, and this new-found situation left me with some time to myself... time to grieve, time to catch up, and time to catch my breath. Going back to work and talking and ministering to people when I was really hurting and in need of someone to minister to me was tough. I am sure anyone in ministry knows what I am talking about, but God sent these great interns at just the right time. Nathan, God is truly very organized! His organization comes from His great love. Nathan also told me to be thankful for Richard and for all that happened, because God says to us; "Rejoice always; pray without ceasing; in everything give thanks; for this is God's will for you in Christ Jesus" (I Thessalonians 5:16-18); that, my friend, is difficult, but OK. And as time went by, I realized just how many miracles God did indeed perform all along the way. I am truly thankful.

Nathan Chesang, 9,000 miles across the ocean, prayed for Richard. I so wanted Richard to be strengthened and to meet Nathan, but they will meet eventually in Heaven. Nathan is a remarkable man. He was a fruit salesman along the side of the road in Kenya. He had no money. He did not have a vehicle and he noticed how those who sold fruit were able to make more money if they had a truck to transport the fruit. He decided that he needed to do something else to earn a living, so he became a welder; after learning the trade, he bought his own equipment and did welding for himself, though still making little money.

One day, he had a friend who told him to sign a piece of paper and that his signature on that paper would make him money. Nathan was buying stock, but had no idea what he was doing as he had never even heard of stocks. He soon forgot all about that piece of paper. Eventually, his friend told him to go to the bank to get his money, though Nathan had no idea how anything worked in the realm of stocks. He was surprised to find out that he made a good amount of money through a single signed piece of paper. Nathan did not understand any of this. While he was at the bank, one of the men who worked in the bank looked through the window of his office and wanted Nathan to come to him. Nathan went into this man's office and was offered a job as a stock broker! He told the man he did not know anything about the business, but this man told Nathan that he would be trained if he wanted the job. He accepted and was trained for a whole two hours! Nathan is now the most trusted man at that bank, and he is doing well financially. He is the chairman of the board of the seminary where I teach annually in Kenya and Nathan is also in charge of a huge ministry called *Circle of Light* in Kenya, which is all over the rest of Africa. He occasionally meets with the former president of Kenya and gives him spiritual advice and guidance. Nathan has no formal higher education, but he has been given an amazing amount of wisdom by God. He is one of the wisest, humblest, and kindest men I know, which is why I wanted him to meet Richard. Those two men had a lot in common as far as their personalities and they would have become instant friends and brothers.

What amazes me about Nathan's story is that God did so much through Nathan, only because he said, "God, use me however you want. I am open to You," and we all need to do the same. How I wonder what Richard would have accomplished through God's Spirit if he had said and done what Nathan did. When we say to God, "Use me wherever You want me to be, and in whatever way You want," be careful. I have prayed that for many years, and though I have no regrets, God used me in a way that caused me great pain and sorrow. Taking care of Richard and watching him die was, by far, the most difficult thing I have ever done, but it was also the most rewarding and fruitful experience of my life. Mother Teresa wrote in her book, *No Greater Love,* that we do not really love until we hurt (Teresa, 1988).

Jesus loved UNTIL it hurt, when He died on the cross and suffered the penalty for our sins, and He continues to love us even when we are disobedient and when we stray, which I believe hurts Him deeply. Jesus loves us, even through the pain we cause Him. He always loves. None of us will ever suffer anywhere close to the degree our Lord Jesus suffered, but love ultimately does bring pain. C.S. Lewis wrote in his famous book *A Grief Observed,* "Bereavement is a universal and integral part of our experience of love" (Lewis, 1966). In any love relationship, someone will usually die before the other, and there will be pain, suffering and bereavement.

When God uses people, sometimes they do not want to go where He wants them to go. Remember Jonah? He did not want to go to Nineveh at all, but that is where God wanted him. Moses did not want to lead all those people, but God chose him. I do not want to fail God in not doing what He calls me to do, even if it hurts. In my selfishness, I would not have wanted to go to the south and suffer the emotional pain and grief of losing a man I deeply loved. However, God wanted me in State X for Richard, and I am eternally thankful for the experience to have loved Richard, and for him to have loved me. Mother Teresa also liked to say, "We cannot all do great things, but we can each do small things with great love." I did a small thing for Richard (in the grand scheme of things) with great love.

Kenya
Nathan is one person in Kenya who had, and still has, a tremendous impact on my spiritual life. There are others as well, such as my friends Kibii and Nebert, and all of the students I have had over the years, some who have even honored me by naming one of their children after me! The main impact Kenya made on me is **the love and care of the people**, especially those in poverty, of which there are many. When there is a need, such as one that comes with a sick person, an orphan, or a widow, there are no discussions about the ability to care for someone financially, if there will be any breach of some man-made ethic, or what someone might think. When a person needs to be cared for in Kenya, one takes care of the need. I have had well-meaning Christian people tell me that this type of action is true for family members, but not for others; I am afraid I do not understand what that means. What do we do with the Richard's of the world who literally have no family, or who have family who will not have anything to do with them? Do we leave them on the street to die alone like the story of the Good Samaritan in Luke 10?

There are a number of passages in the Bible that refer to widows. In I Timothy 5:3 Paul mentions widows "who are really widows." What is the definition of one who is "really a widow"? A "widow" is a person who literally has no one. While Richard did have a niece, she had nothing to do with him, and even after she was eventually contacted by the hospital and told that he had terminal cancer, she told the doctors to do whatever they thought best, as she did not want to get involved. Had Richard known such a discussion took place, I cannot even imagine the hurt he would have felt, especially since he told me several times how much he loved his niece. In a matter of speaking, Richard was like one who is really a widow. I believe I Timothy 5:3 can and does refer to all people who are alone, and that this passage is not necessarily limited to a woman whose husband died and who is childless and without any family. There are many "widows" in the world, like Richard. There are many orphans, who can also be defined as weak, sick people without parents or family. Richard was sixty years old, but when he was sick, weak, and literally dying, he was as dependant as a child and unable to care for himself. Richard was both an orphan and a widow. Paul also wrote in I Timothy 5:8, "And whoever does not provide for relatives, and especially family members, has denied the faith and is worse than an unbeliever." We are all part of the family of God, which would make Richard a relative to us all. My Kenyan brothers and sisters are my relatives, and they always treated me as such, and I am sure they understand that verse in this context as well.

One year when I was in Kenya, the weather was cooler than I had prepared for, and I did not have a jacket. One rainy afternoon, when the sun was gone and the temperature dropped, one of my students (named Rose) gave me her woolen shawl to wear, which I greatly appreciated. I assumed she gave it to me for the few weeks that I would be there, which was a huge sacrifice in itself, so on the day that I was to leave I went to give it back to her with my thanks. Rose looked at me strangely and told me it was now mine. She GAVE the shawl to me. She saw a need, and she met it. There was no ethical question as to whether or not a teacher could accept a gift from a student, like at the hospital where an employee is not allowed to accept a gift from a patient; such an idea would have been so foreign to Rose and to my other friends in Kenya. One simply does what needs to be done, and one gives when there is a need.

In Kenya, there are no nursing homes or institutions where people are sent to die. Family members care for the dying, and if there are no family members, which would be rare, then the community or Church takes care of them, without question. When I emailed Nathan and other friends in Kenya to ask them to please pray for Richard whom I was caring for, there was never a question as to whether or not I should have him in my home. No one asked me if this course of action was appropriate or not, nor would they have even imagined that I broke any ethical boundaries in the hospital. Thoughts such as these would appear crazy in Kenya, and in my mind, they ARE crazy!

A former student of mine in Kenya, John, was a pastor who took in several orphans to live in his home, even though he had no money or room for them. No one in his church would even consider whether or not a pastor should do this, as they would not question my choice in taking Richard in to help him in his final months. The thoughts and so-called "rules" we Americans make are quite foreign and even barbaric to many people in the world. We affluent, comfortable Westerners foolishly consider such caring, compassionate foreigners to be "uncivilized." It's funny, but my Kenyan friends would consider our ethical boundaries and lack of care for the Richard's of the world to be quite uncivilized, as indeed such indifference is. We have much to learn from what are falsely called "backward" and "uncivilized third-world countries."

Grief

Living with the pain of losing Richard, especially after such a brief time together, caused all kinds of theological dilemmas for me. While I was reading *A Grief Observed,* about the death of C.S. Lewis' wife, he wrote an interesting section. In pondering his marriage and the loss of his wife, Lewis wrote,

It was too perfect to last, so I am tempted to say about our marriage. But it can be meant in two ways. It may be grimly pessimistic – as if God no sooner saw two of His creatures happy than He stopped it ('None of that here!'). As if He were like the Hostess at the sherry-party who separates two guests the moment they show signs of having got into a real conversation. But it could also mean 'This had reached its proper perfection. This had become what it had in it to be.' Therefore of course it would not be prolonged. As if God said, 'Good; you have mastered that exercise. I am pleased with it. And now you are ready to go on to the next... The teacher moves you on' (Lewis, 1966).

I felt not that first scenario, but the second when Richard died, when I clearly heard God tell me, when I first woke up and saw that Richard was gone, "You did what I sent you here to do." The exercise was finished; it was time to go on to the next. It was just unbelievably painful.

Richard was dying. I had to face that fact, though we preferred for the most part not to. We used to tell one another that the only way we could deal with his immanent death was to ignore it, as if it would go away, almost like the "ignorance is bliss" attitude. A little denial kept us sane. When Richard first came to live with me, we often discussed his illness and impending death. We prepared and made sure he was "ready" to meet his Lord and Savior, and we said all the things between us that needed to be said. Yet, after a while, Richard said those conversations were depressing him too much, and he no longer wanted to talk about his death. When all of his affairs were in order, I said, "Alright... we don't have to talk about that anymore. Let's focus on living," and that is all we did.

Richard admitted to me that he had overdosed many other times, besides his one overdose in my apartment. He could have easily died, like so many people do, at any one of those times. He was almost dead when he came into the hospital back in November when I first ran into him, shortly after his first and only round of chemotherapy in October. He almost died when he had sepsis in late November/early December, but he did not. God's mercy was so great that He waited for Richard to get his spiritual life in order, to come back to Him, and to be the man he was supposed to be all along, before he died. I was merely the person used to help bring him back around and to show him the love of Christ; for that privilege, I will be forever grateful.

At one point during my care for Richard, when I was becoming quite weary with grief, I asked God, "Why Me? Why didn't You send someone else to take care of Richard? This is just too hard!" But I would not have it any other way. I am so thankful that God brought Richard and I together and showed both of us so many things about who He is and the sheer power of human love. I always prayed at breakfast, and Richard prayed at dinner. I usually prayed a prayer of thanksgiving for another day of life, for Richard being in my life, and for God to help us to love one another, to love Him more perfectly, and to live in ways that reflected such a love. I also prayed for safety and protection over Richard for the day.

On an occasion or two, I told Richard that I must love him more than I realized, since I would have never put up with half of what I put up with for anyone else! I put up with his morphine abuse for over a month, which I found repulsive. I prayed about it so many days and nights, and God told me not to give up on Richard, but that I should keep on loving him as He loves us. We all were, at one time, that one lost sheep out of the 100 whom God searched for and found. Many of us were that Prodigal Son in whom all of Heaven rejoiced when he finally came to his senses. Love is much more than that warm, fuzzy feeling we get. It is much more than an emotion. Love is a verb as well as a noun. It is an act of the will that God commands (Leviticus 19:18; Matthew 19:19). I was told to love Richard, and God gave me the strength to love him, until I actually did fall deeply in love with him, and he with me. We loved. It was as simple as that. And God, not me, changed Richard.

There will be many things on earth we never understand. Why did Richard live the life that he did? Why did he have to suffer, and why did I have to feel so much pain and loss? As C.S. Lewis wrote in *A Grief Observed*, "When I lay these questions before God I get no answer. But a rather special sort of 'No answer.' It is not the locked door. It is more like a silent, certainly not uncompassionate, gaze. As though He shook His head not in refusal but waiving the question, Like, 'Peace, child; you don't understand'" (Lewis, 1966).

There are many things in this life we may never understand. God often works in seemingly strange ways, according to human standards. When Jesus lived on earth, He lived outside of the norms of society by following the Scriptures. I believe God did, and still does, act in those kinds of ways. I had a few people (not many) who thought it was awful and just plain sinful that I should have a man who was not my husband live with me. Though I had received confirmation over and over that this is what God wanted me to do, I was still sometimes criticized. Richard and I had a very close and intimate relationship, but we did not commit any sin the

Bible speaks about. I prayed about my decision daily to take Richard in, and was confirmed over and over. There is no sin in taking care of a dying person of the opposite sex. There is no sin in a woman loving a man until literal death. Jesus went against many of the "rules" and norms of society, and He will, at times, tell us to do the same. I have no regrets.

I was also told by some that there are a lot of people who have no family and who die alone, and I cannot take them all in; I have no intention of doing so. I believe that God brought me to the Veteran's hospital in order to take care of Richard. He did not bring me there to take care of the world. Each person is unique and special to God and, for whatever reason, God chose me to care for Richard. That is all I know, and I tried my best to be obedient to His call. God may never tell me to do such a thing for someone again, and I have no way to know right now, but I do know that we are to obey God over man (Acts 4:13-20). When I believed God called me to do something, I needed to listen and obey, despite some criticisms. Obedience is not an option, even when it might not make sense to us. Several people also told me that I could lose my job for taking Richard home with me. For me, no job is as important as a human life, so if that were to happen, so be it; however, I was sure that I would not lose my job, and of course, I did not.

Did God want to hurt me and to bring me the great pain and grief I feel today? No. I serve a loving God. Love is sacrifice, and my love was a sacrifice for Richard who needed someone to love him and care for him. He needed someone to live with him and to help him die. Someone had to do it... so why not me? Why not you? Love is a verb as well as a noun; love is an act of the will as much as it is a perception of the heart. Love is a sacrifice that we make for others with no concern for what it does to us. It is for the benefit of others, yet in a mysterious way, God brings us joy in the midst of that sacrifice and great growth. There is no growth without pain, and the greater the growth, the greater the pain; the greater the love, the greater the loss. Truly, it is better to have loved and lost, than never to have loved at all (*In Memoriam,* Tennyson). I am thankful to have loved Richard, and for him to have died knowing he was deeply loved.

Richard's death has left an incredible void in my life. Our relationship was short but intensely close and it ended in death. I go through waves of unbelievable pain of missing him. I long so much to see him and touch him, to talk to him, to hold him, and to kiss him. While some of you may be thinking our relationship was so short, at the same time it was intense. It was a struggle for survival and for love. It was filled with hopes that never materialized. I literally took care of every square inch of this man's body when he was dying, such as cutting his finger and toe nails, shaving his face and trimming his mustache, helping him bathe, washing his feet, changing his diaper, etc. For the first time in his life, Richard exposed his heart and his soul, and he trusted another human being – me. Love is incredibly powerful and intense. We must have the capacity to always give and receive love to know God. C.S. Lewis wrote in his book *A Grief Observed,* "You must have the capacity to receive, or even omnipotence can't give" (Lewis, 1966).

The Foolish and the Wise
Jesus did many socially unacceptable things in the course of His ministry that many considered taboo, like talking to women, eating and hanging out with tax collectors and prostitutes, touching sick people, healing on the Sabbath and so forth. Those social taboos that Jesus broke were actually unscriptural, as they prohibited real love and respect for all people. Because Jesus did these unusual things while He was here to teach the "religious" people of His day the way to really live, I believe God also calls us to do some unusual

things as well. For instance, I, the chaplain, came to serve and wash the feet of a social outcast whom many looked upon as one of the "least of these," and it was me, more than Richard, who learned so much through this incredibly spiritual experience. "But God chose what is foolish in the world to shame the wise; God chose what is weak in the world to shame the strong; God chose what is low and despised in the world, things that are not, to reduce to nothing things that are, so that no one might boast in the presence of God" (I Corinthians 1:28-29). Richard shamed me by exposing my own errant attitudes, and he taught me a great deal about God's love, mercy, and forgiveness, and about human love; I will live by these lessons forever.

Since my job with the Veterans hospital was only a one-year contract, it had to end. A big concern to some of the chaplains was that I may have "crossed a boundary" that professionally should not have been crossed by taking Richard to my home. Where is the concern about the life and death of a human being? I am looked upon with suspicion for having done such a thing; I must admit complete and utter amazement at such an attitude. I cannot imagine Jesus telling me, "Donna, let Richard die alone without ever experiencing true love and tenderness from another human being. Don't you dare let him learn what it means to trust another person completely, and Heaven forbid that he sees the love of Jesus at work in the life of one who can love him unconditionally. There are rules to follow that the hospital administration made, where people who have no family must die alone in the institutions provided. Chaplains and Christ-followers must leave them alone, and if they die without love, at least the man-made rules were followed and there was no societal breach."

Had Richard been given a court-appointed guardian and gone into an institutional Hospice center alone, as was suggested, I do not believe that he would have come to the spiritual place in his life that he did, and he would have missed out on the experience of unconditional love and trust. The attitude of those who so often receive the greatest respect (such as the chaplains, supervisors, administrators, and those supposedly in-the-know) is quite repulsive to me, and I believe this attitude is also repulsive to Christ. Man-made rules should never supersede the love and care for another human being. As I believe with all of my heart that God wanted me to take care of Richard (and I did) God also did indeed provide another chaplain position for me that followed the end of my contract at the Veterans' hospital. In this new hospital, the chaplain staff was aware of the circumstances that surrounded Richard and I, and they were grateful for our experience and were happy to welcome me aboard.

Dr. Wess Stafford, President and CEO of Compassion International, wrote in his book *Too Small to Ignore: Why the Least of These Matter* that, "Every human being needs a cause in life, a passion. If you don't have something that makes your heart pound, that can move you to tears of joy or tears of sorrow in about thirty seconds, then my friend, you are not fully alive," (Stafford, 2007). The "least of these" are the children, whom Dr. Stafford works hard for and has dedicated his life to. The "least of these" are also people like Richard, who have no one to speak up for them, who have no family, no resources, no hope, and who are weak, sick and dying... people who are completely dependant on other human beings, just as children are completely dependant. I believe we must do all we can for people such as Richard, and I think worrying about man-made rules that run counter to the Scriptures surely breaks the heart of God. We humans often just don't get it.

Time
Scripture tells of time. Time was created by God in Genesis with the creation of the sun, moon and stars. "Then God said,

Let there be lights in the firmament of the heaven to separate the day from the night; and let them be for signs, and for seasons, and for days, and years" (Genesis 1:14).

Scripture also tells of how our finite, earthly time differs from God's time; " But do not ignore this one fact, beloved, that with the Lord one day is like a thousand years, and a thousand years are like one day. The Lord is not slow about His promise, as some think of slowness, but is patient with you, not wanting any to perish, but all to come to repentance." (2 Peter 3:8-9). This verse from 2 Peter speaks of the patience of God in desiring all people to come to Him for their salvation. When Richard mentioned to me that he lived longer than the rest of his family, I reminded him of this gracious fact. God is truly good and loving with time.

My time with Richard seemed to be outside of the box. I felt like I lived a life time in ten short months. What encompasses many lives? You meet someone, fall in love, get married, and one partner usually dies first, leaving the other to grieve the loss. These events normally take place over many years, or a life time. Though Richard and I never married, he lived with me in the final months of his life, and we went through the same life time experiences together, though in the rapid pace of ten short months. It was delightful, yet exhausting to live a life time in under a year!

Love and Eternity
I will always love God. I will always love Richard and I will always be grateful that God brought me into Richard's life in order to let him die and be mourned and remembered with Christian love and dignity. Some day, my ashes will be scattered with Richard's in some beautiful place, and I will see Richard again in Heaven. I used to always tell Richard that there is no time in Heaven (Isaiah 60:19-20; Revelation 21:23), and I hope that when I get there, he will be on his horse, turn and look,

and we'll be together again. While we are lonely and miss those we love on earth after they die, we have their memories and their love, rooted in Christ, whom our loved ones are seeing face to face when they go to Heaven. Romans 8:35-39 says, "Who can separate us from the love of Christ? Will hardship, or distress, or persecution, or famine, or sword? As it is written, 'For our sake we are being killed all day long; we are accounted as sheep to be slaughtered.' No, in all things we are more than conquerors through him who loved us. For I am convinced that neither death, nor life, nor angels, nor rulers, nor things present, nor things to come, nor powers, nor height, nor depth, nor anything else in all creation, will be able to separate us from the love of God in Christ Jesus our Lord."

> **"See, the home of God is among mortals. He will dwell with them; they will be His peoples, and God Himself will wipe every tear from their eyes. Death will be no more; mourning and crying and pain will be no more"**
> **–Revelation 21:3-4**

Chapter Eight

Thinking Outside the Box

A wise man told me that God works outside the box. After reflection, I agree. I began this book by stating that I think outside the box. Do not misunderstand – I am not comparing myself to God. I believe that when we are open minded God will cause us to think outside the box, since He works in ways that are generally contrary to human reasoning and actions. Scripture is clear: "Do not be conformed to this world, but be transformed by the renewing of your minds, so that you may discern what is the will of God – what is good and acceptable and perfect" (Romans 12:2).

Think and Work Outside the Box
Discerning the will of God can be perplexing. We often hear what we want to hear and question those ideas, thoughts and actions that appear illogical or difficult, but more often than not are indeed the will of God. Human nature naturally resists, but through the renewing of our minds and the power of the Holy Spirit, we can think and work outside the box with God, and watch the plans of God unfold. Of course, having the eyes to see God's plan is always much easier in retrospect!

The entire Christian message is outside the box. Think about the fact that God left the glory of Heaven to come to earth as a poor, basically homeless tradesman, born outside in a barn to an unmarried virgin woman, and willingly allowed Himself to be tortured to death, all for the sake of His great love for humanity. What about the lessons from the Sermon on the Mount as recorded in Matthew 5-7? Isn't turning the other cheek, loving our enemies, and praying for those who persecute us thinking outside the box? What about losing your life so you can find/save it? What about the idea of hating this world, along with the money and material possessions in it, for the sake of loving God instead and willingly becoming poor so as to gain wealth in Heaven; is this idea not outside of normal human pursuits? What about in the Old Testament, when God used a small young shepherd boy like David to defeat the mightiest, strongest, most feared man like Goliath, and then had this shepherd become the greatest king Israel ever had in order to show His power and who is really the true King? God often uses people who the world would never consider "worthy" to be used, for His purposes and to show His power, love and glory. God was able to use a single, uneducated, teenage mom like me, but only after I finally submitted to Him and learned to let go of my own destructive ways. I could give example after example... Yes, God does think outside the box.

God's Chess Game
The primary focus of this book was to show God's amazing love and grace, which He displayed in the life and death of Richard. There was another focus as well which reflects God's love; God's ways are not our ways – they are so much greater, so surprising, and so fulfilling, even in the midst of pain. Blackaby's study entitled *Experiencing God* repeatedly mentions how God moves us and guides us in unusual ways, outside the box so to speak, to accomplish His will.

I look at life and the movements of God as a cosmic universal chess game, with God moving the pieces around to accomplish His eventual checkmate. This analogy is a way for me to try to grasp a small portion of the infinite mind of God and to help me navigate through the uncertainties of life and to discern His will. I do not think life is a big game, but I believe, as in chess, we have to be willing to take risks and make moves that at the moment, especially to those who do not understand the game of chess, seemingly make no sense, but have a strategy and purpose for eventual gain and accomplishment. We need to be willing to be God's pawns, to step out in faith, to advance forward onto those two squares on that first move, and to open ourselves up for capture, while we realize that our protection and power lies in the King who is always keeping a close watch on our moves. I also believe we take ourselves far too seriously, and we need to be willing to play a lot more in this great game of chess, with a greater spirit of adventure which I think God wants us to enjoy. Jesus already took life and death seriously when He came as our sacrifice to teach us how to live and love. I think we can live life with great love and sensitivity, but realize that we can laugh at ourselves, enjoy others, and move with a spirit of risk and wonder, and walk outside the box as God leads.

My Story

I began this book with some background information about myself and the uncertain moves that surrounded my life at the completion of my seminary training and some of the events that followed for the next few years. I allowed you, my readers, into my story to show you my personal resistance and uncertainties of what life was bringing, my faith struggles, and my questioning of God when times got hard and life seemed to make no sense and have no direction; it was in those places that God was working, preparing me and building my faith. How easy to see God work when it's all said and done!

How difficult it is to trust and obey in the heat of battle! I was hoping to show the "game of chess" God was playing, so to speak, in the movements of my life and how God's ways were never my ways, but accomplished that which could never be accomplished left to my human reasoning and pride.

I lived the first 44 years of my life in the Chicago area. Chicago is a major metropolitan northern part of the United States, which is far different from rural Kentucky. I then moved farther south to State X, where I never thought I would live. I worked in the construction business for over twenty years, which, as a woman, is "outside the box", only to then work in an office for a year in Kentucky. I moved to Kentucky to work on my Doctorate, only to find myself on my hands and knees in the dirt pulling weeds as a landscaper, and feeding pigs on a farm, perhaps so that I would become more humble and able to serve, and allow God to chip away at my pride, which is always sneaking up on me. Our pursuits and goals are often contrary to God's call on our lives, and we often find that His call is much more in-line with who we are than our own ideas about ourselves. God knows us better then we know ourselves.

I moved from the financial and personal comfort and stability of my house to living alone for the first time in a strange new state in an apartment. I left home, while my son remained in the family house. I went from thinking that I was working as a chaplain to serve and to teach my patients God's love, as one educated and trained for ministry, only to discover that I would learn incredible lessons from one of the "least of these" (namely Richard) who showed me God's unconditional love and forgiveness. I learned and received from Richard, and from many of my patients, much more than I could offer to them. In my story, I hope you can understand, as I am learning with each day, that God does indeed think and work outside our box. When life seems to make no sense to us at all, that is when He is hard at work in our lives, moving us around this giant chessboard. It is in these difficult moments that we need to pay attention.

Discontentment as a Chess Move
The apostle Paul wrote, "I have learned to be content with whatever I have. I know what it is to have little, and I know what it is to have plenty. In any and all circumstances I have learned the secret of being well-fed and of going hungry, of having plenty and of being in need. I can do all things through Him who strengthens me" (Philippians 4:11b-13). However, I believe we can be discontented in order to cause us to act, but within that discontentment, we can be content in the knowledge and assurance that God is at work and remains faithful to His Word.

Had I not been unhappy and discontent in my work in Kentucky, I would never have thought to move away to where Richard lived. Richard needed me to care for him, and he needed to learn more of God's grace and compassion. From a human perspective, it made more sense to stay in the area where I had a house, rather than look for work elsewhere and go live in an apartment. God can use any type of circumstance, including unhappiness or discontentment for His plans; "We know that all things work together for good for those who love God, who are called according to His purpose" (Romans 8:28). "All things", can sometimes include unhappiness and dissatisfaction.

Ultimate Contentment and Assurance
Our greatest and ultimate learning, I believe, often lies in the contentment of temporary unhappiness, knowing that God can fulfill in us what He wants us to do, that He can make us who He wants us to be, and that we must be willing to go where He leads – easier said than done. The journey is often lonely and difficult, but God promises never to leave or forsake

us. The apostle Paul wrote in his letter in II Corinthians 4:8-10 and 17-18, "We are afflicted in every way, but not crushed; perplexed, but not driven to despair; persecuted, but not forsaken; struck down, but not destroyed... For this slight momentary affliction is preparing us for an eternal weight of glory beyond all measure, because we look not at what can be seen but at what cannot be seen; for what can be seen is temporary, but what cannot be seen is eternal."

God never promised us an easy journey, but He promised us joy in Him, meaning and purpose in life, and fulfillment that the world can never give. God thinks way outside our box, and invites us to as well. The amazement, joy, love, and wonder in life comes in following Christ and walking outside the box as He leads, which can sometimes be frightening. Richard and I walked outside the box together, and found love and truth that we would never have otherwise. Life was incredibly difficult and painful for us both at times, especially near the end of Richard's life, but we had assurance in the Word of God, as spoken to Joshua in the Old Testament:

> **"As I was with Moses, so I will be with you; I will not fail you or forsake you. Be strong and courageous"**
>
> **--Joshua 1:5**

References

Blackaby, Henry and Richard. *Experiencing God.* Nashville, Tennessee: LifeWay Press, 2007.

Benner, David G. *Care of Souls.* Grand Rapids, Michigan: Baker Books, 1998.

Brother Lawrence. *The Practice of the Presence of God.* Ohio,
Barbour, Value Books, 2004.

Cowen, James A. *When it's All Been Said and Done.* Integrity Music, 1999.

Lewis, C. S. *A Grief Observed.* San Francisco, California: Harper Collins, 1966.

Lewis, C. S. *The Problem of Pain.* New York: Macmillan Publishing Company, 1962.

Mother Teresa. *No Greater Love.* Novato, California: New World Library, 1989.

Nouwen, Henri J.M. *With Burning Hearts: A Meditation on the Eucharistic Life.* Mary Knoll, New York: Orbis Books, 1994.

Parent, Marc. *Turning Stones: My Days and Nights with Children at Risk.* New York: Harcourt Brace and Company, 1996.

Siegal, Bernie M.D. *Peace, Love and Healing.* Flint, Michigan: Arrow Publishing, 1991.

Stafford, Dr. Wess. *Too Small to Ignore: Why the Least of These Matters the Most.* Colorado Springs, Colorado: WaterBrook Press, 2007.

Tennyson, Alfred Lord. *In Memoriam:27,* 1850.

Holy Bible from the Ancient Eastern Text. George M. Lamsa's Translation, San Francisco: Harper Collins Publishers, 1968.

The New Oxford Annotated Bible. New York: Oxford University Press. 1989.

Post Script

Home at Last Animal Sanctuary

Home at Last Animal Sanctuary is the farm where I worked in Kentucky, owned and run by Margie and Terry. It is accredited by the American Sanctuary Association and provides care for many animals, including cats, dogs, cows, pigs, and goats and includes a separate wildlife refuge. It is a no-kill sanctuary emphasizing the concept of compassion and offering exceptional quality of life for many formerly abandoned or abused animals.

All contributions to *Home at Last* are tax deductible. If you would like to find out more about this animal sanctuary, and/or make a contribution, you may contact them at P.O. Box 144, Salvisa, KY 40372 or look them up on the web at www.homeatlastanimals.org.

Thinking Outside the Box About Love
ISBN 978-1-935434-00-9

GreenWine Family Books™
A division of GlobalEdAdvancePress
www.globaledadvance.org

www.ingramcontent.com/pod-product-compliance
Lightning Source LLC
Chambersburg PA
CBHW071710090426
42738CB00009B/1725